Sarah M Howell and Lisa Kester-Dod

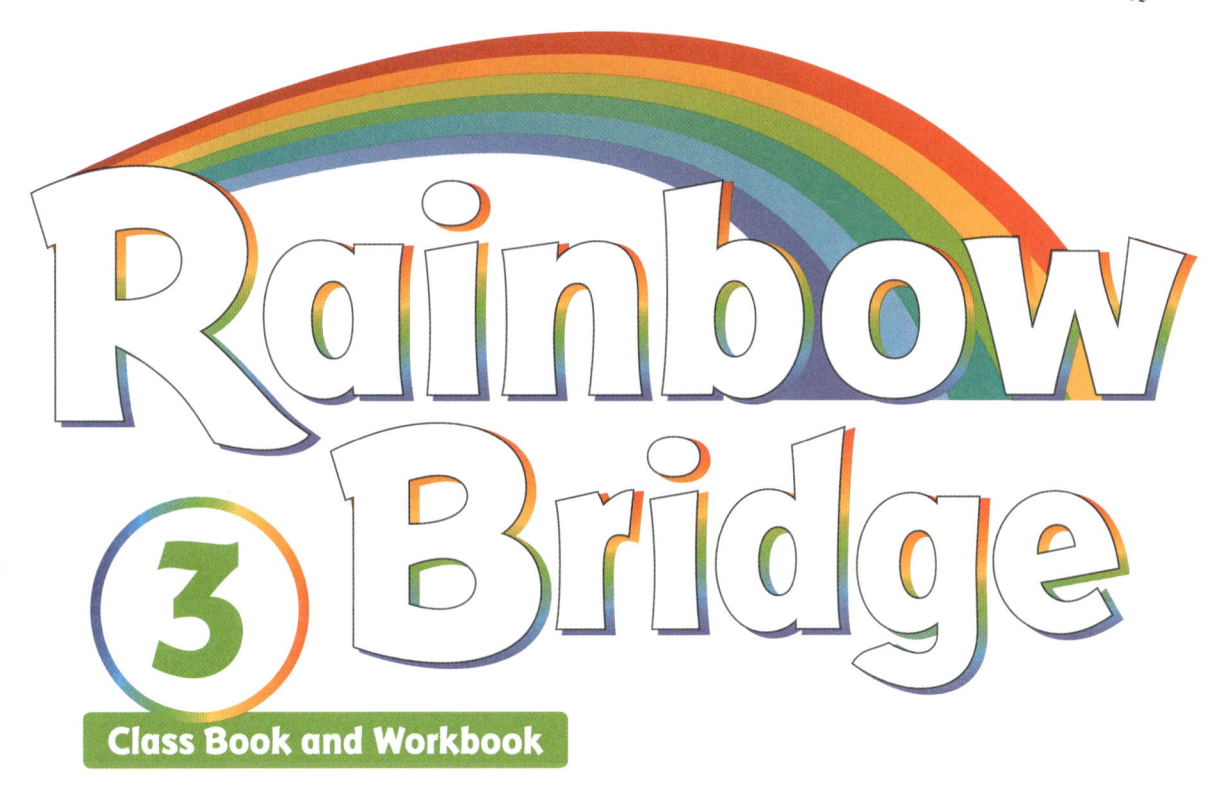

Rainbow Bridge 3
Class Book and Workbook

Class Book

Around Bridge Town

Along the canal — 4
Unit 1 In the town — 6
Unit 2 Numbers — 14

At the station — 22
Unit 3 Food and drink — 24
Unit 4 At the shop — 32

In the woods — 40
Unit 5 My bedroom — 42
Unit 6 Playtime — 50

At the beach — 58
Unit 7 Clothes — 60
Unit 8 Sports — 68

CLIL Science: The water cycle — 76
CLIL Science: Healthy eating — 78
CLIL Citizenship: Recycling — 80
CLIL Geography: Landscapes — 82
Culture: Food and me! — 84
Culture: Sport and dance and me! — 86
Festivals: It's Christmas Eve! — 88
Festivals: It's Easter time! — 89

Workbook

Unit 1 In the town — 90
Unit 2 Numbers — 93
Unit 3 Food and drink — 96
Unit 4 At the shop — 99
Unit 5 My bedroom — 102
Unit 6 Playtime — 105
Unit 7 Clothes — 108
Unit 8 Sports — 111

Extra grammar practice

Unit 1 — 114
Unit 2 — 115
Unit 3 — 116
Unit 4 — 117
Unit 5 — 118
Unit 6 — 119
Unit 7 — 120
Unit 8 — 121

Wordlist — 122
Song lyrics — 124

OXFORD

Sid

Dickin

Rowan

Poppy

Will

Emily

Sniff

Fern

Russ

Along the canal

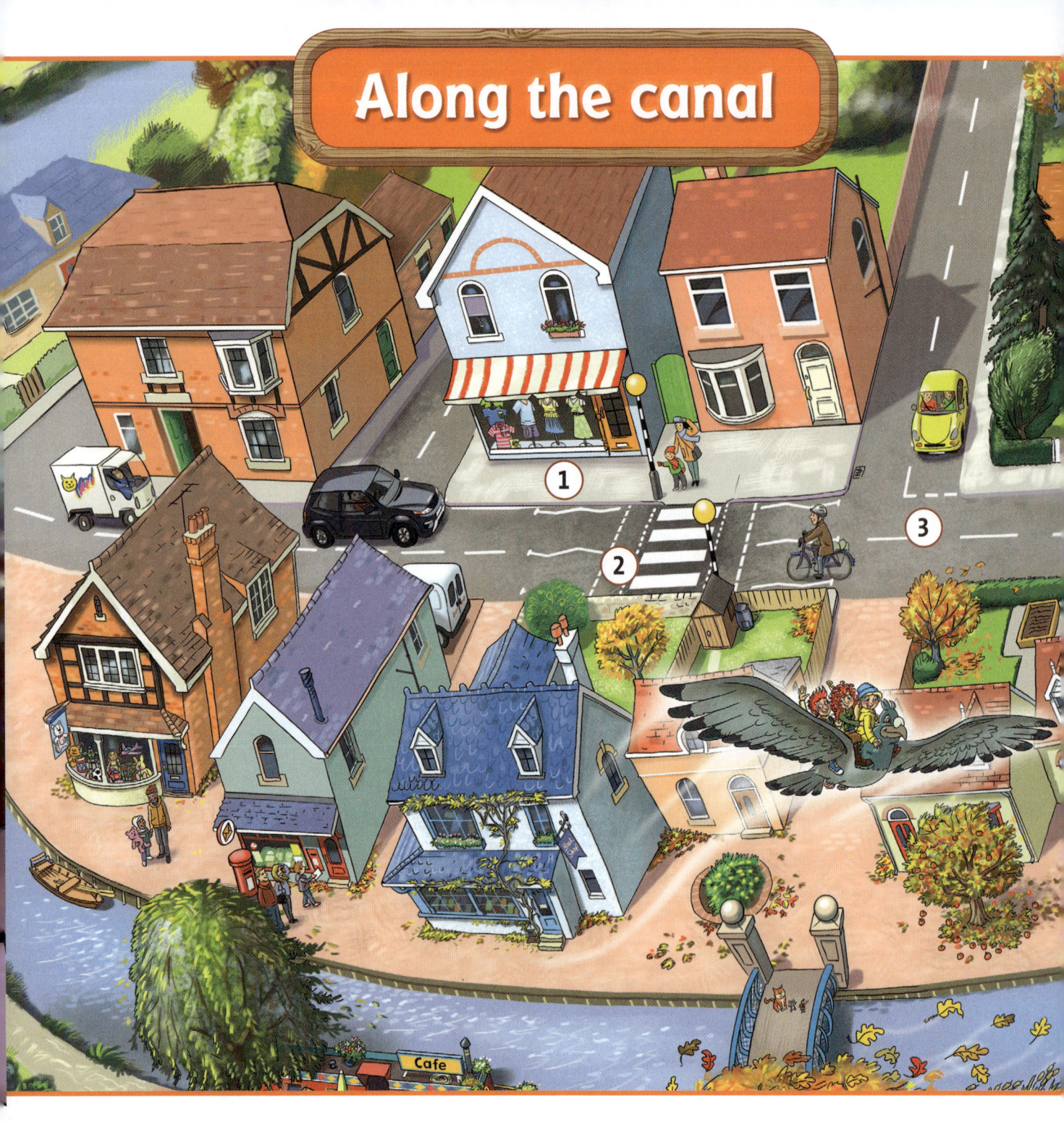

1 Watch the video. ▶

2 (Think) Talk about Bridge Town. *See TG notes.*

3 Listen and point. Repeat. Write. 🔊 1.1–1.2

> a zebra crossing   a road   a traffic light
> a seat belt   a helmet   the pavement

1 _____   2 _____   3 _____

4 _____   5 _____   6 _____

4

Units 1–2 Road safety

4 Sing *The Road Safety Song*. 🔊 1.3–1.4

Look left, look right.
Wait for the traffic lights
To change from red to green.
Be cool, be great.
Stop. Look. Listen. Wait!
When you cross the road.

Walk on the pavement
When you're in the town.
Keep safe, be cool.
Always look around.

Put on a seat belt
When you're in a car.
Keep safe, be cool.
You're a superstar!

5 Class project Make a Road Safety poster. *See TG notes.*

6 The story so far Listen and answer the questions. 🔊 1.5 *See TG notes.*

a zebra crossing, a road, a traffic light, a seat belt, a helmet, the pavement
Look left. Look right. Stop. Look. Listen. Wait!

🎵 p124

1 In the town — Lesson 1

1 Listen and point. Repeat. Number. 🔊 1.6–1.7

2 *Think* Talk about your town. See TG notes.

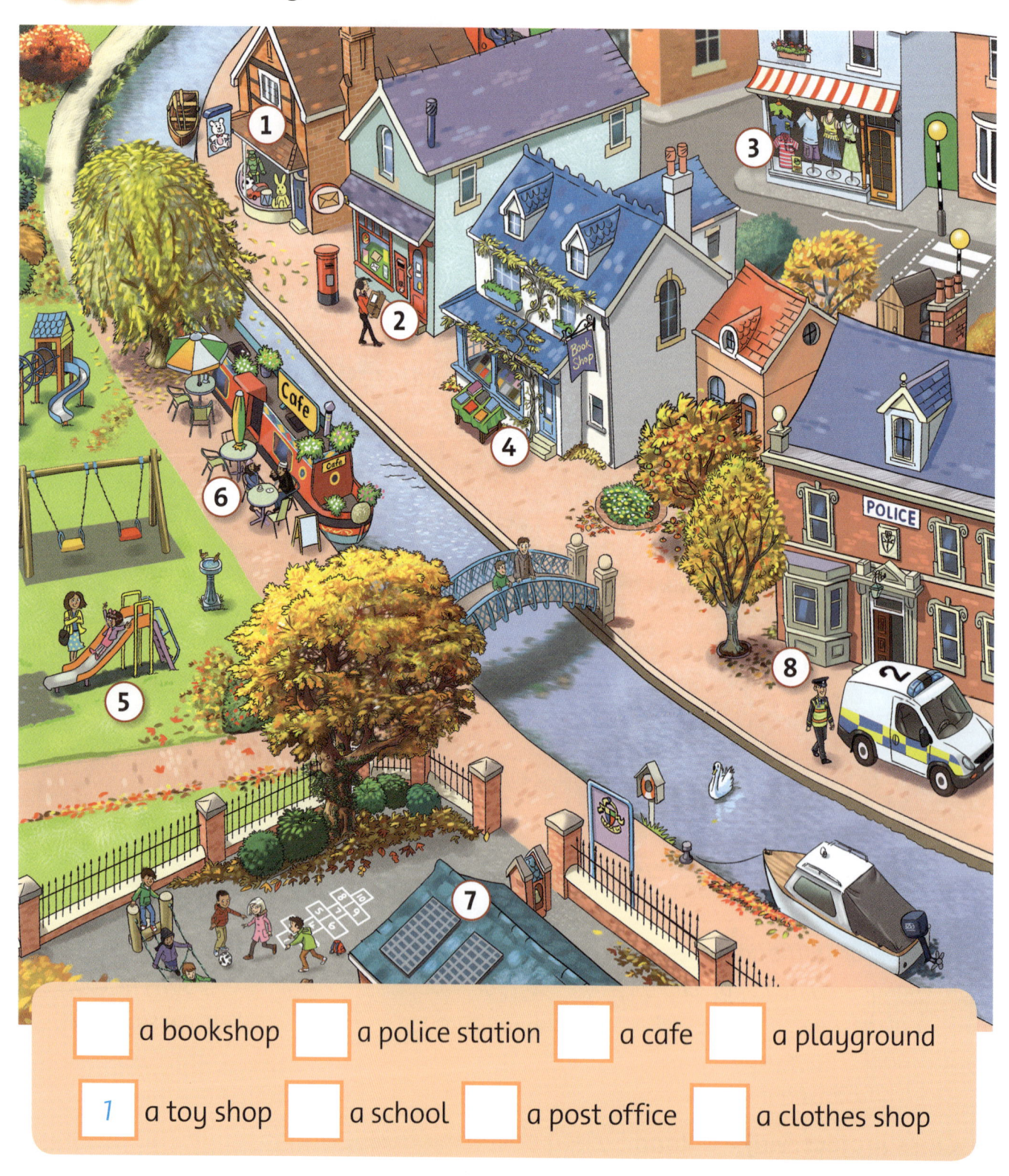

☐ a bookshop ☐ a police station ☐ a cafe ☐ a playground

[1] a toy shop ☐ a school ☐ a post office ☐ a clothes shop

3 Chant. 🔊 1.8

4 Play *The Questions Game*. See TG notes.

6 — a bookshop, a police station, a cafe, a playground, a toy shop, a school, a post office, a clothes shop — p 90

Lesson 2

1 Write and say.

2 Sing the *Let's go to Town Song*. 1.9–1.10

Hello, nice to meet you!
How are you today?
Welcome to my busy town.
Let me show you around.

Look, there's a post office
A police station, too.
Look, there's a toy shop
Just for you.
Look, there's a school
And lots of cafes.
There are lots of playgrounds.
I play with my friends all day.

a bookshop, a police station, a cafe, a playground, a toy shop, a school, a post office, a clothes shop

p124 p90

7

1 Lesson 3 Come back!

1 (Think) Listen. Where's the story? 🔊 1.11 See TG notes.

2 Now watch or listen and read. ▶ 🔊 1.12

1 I'm bored. Let's go to town.

2 I've got my bike. Come on!

3 Look, there's a police station. There are lots of leaves!

4 There's a playground. Uh oh. It's my sister! Hide!

5 What's this? No, stop, Emily!

6 Aargh! Jump!

7 Poppy, no!

I'm bored. Let's go to town. Hide! Jump! Is it the cafe? No, it isn't! Come back!

Lesson 4

8 — Oh no! Where's Russ? / Look! Is it the cafe?

9 — Er... No, it isn't! / Come back!

1 Write. Number the story in order.

What   Come   town

_____ back!

Let's go to _____.

_____'s this?

2 Who is calm? Look and tick (✓).

3 (Think) Talk about being calm. *See TG notes.*

p 91

Lesson 5

1 Listen and repeat. Then say. 🔊 1.13

There's a school.

There are three bikes.

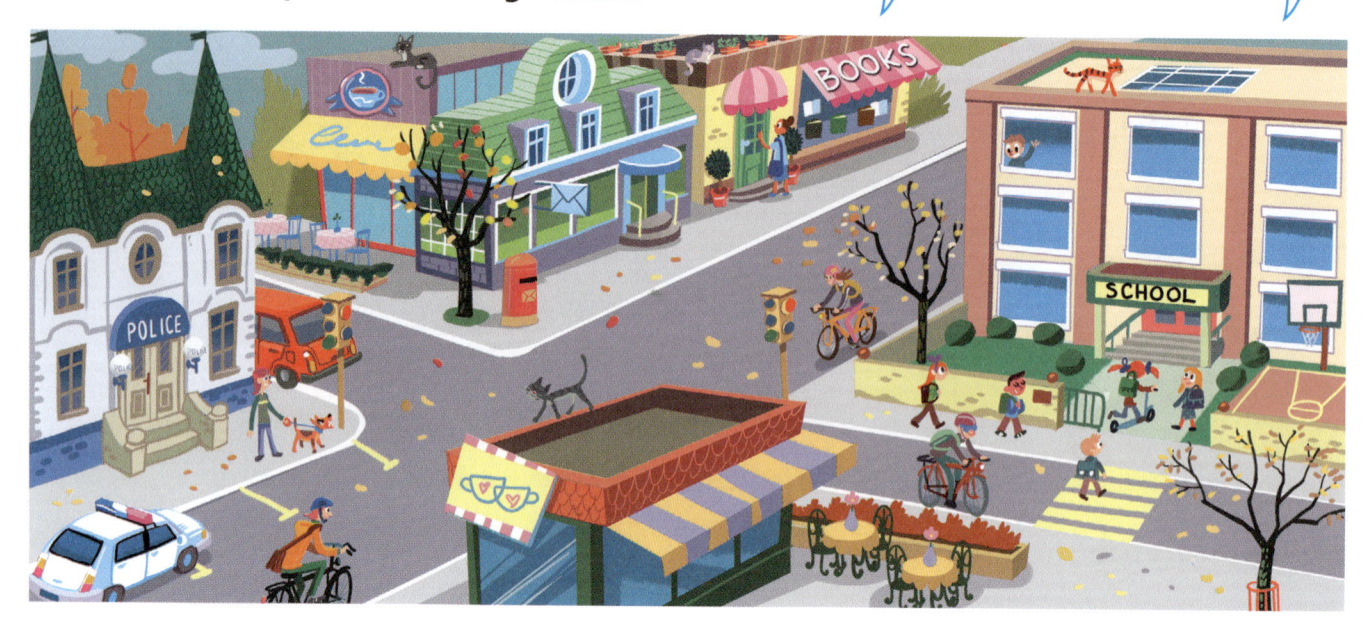

2 Write *There's a* or *There are*.

1 _____There's a_____ school.
2 _____There are_____ three bikes.
3 _____ two cafes.
4 _____ lots of leaves.
5 _____ bookshop.
6 _____ post office.

3 What's different? Look and say.

There's a playground.

There are two playgrounds.

There's a school. There are three bikes. There are lots of leaves.

Grammar p 114   p 92

10

Lesson 6

1 Listen and tick (✓). Then draw, tick (✓) and say. 🔊 1.14

Me

2 Write an email. Draw a picture of your town.

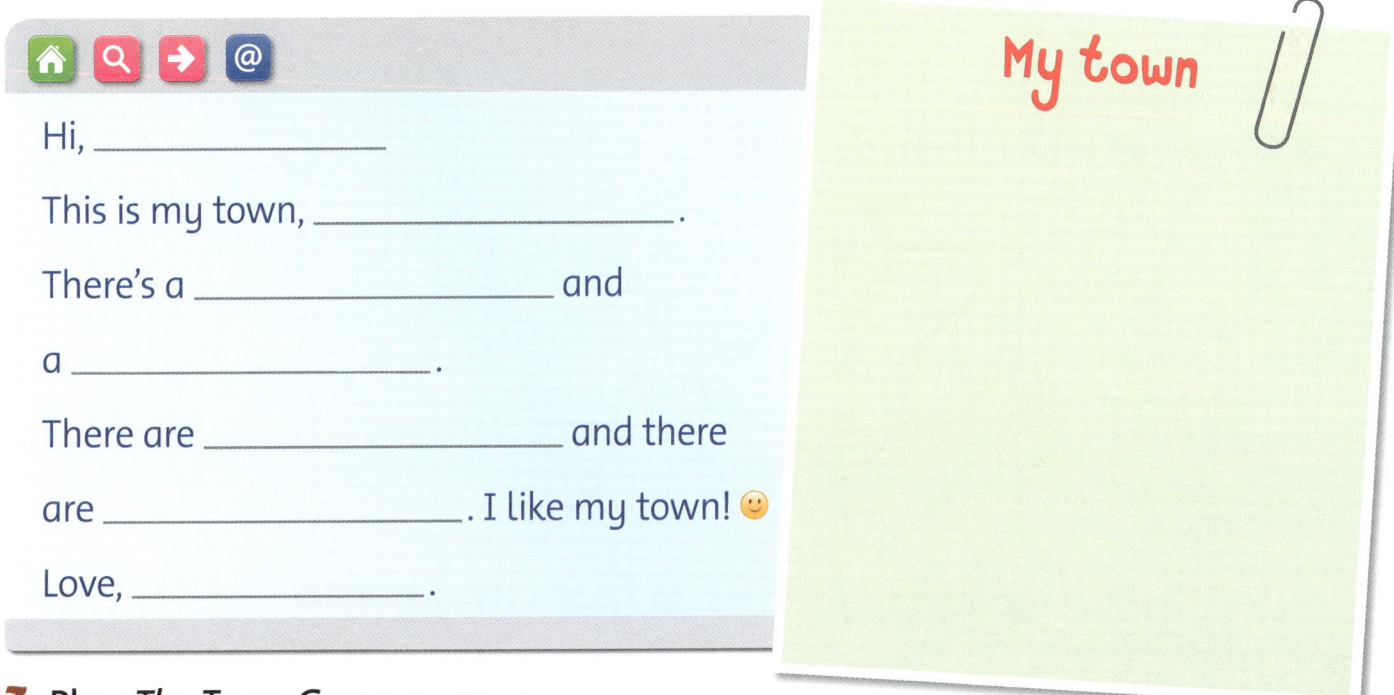

Hi, _____

This is my town, _____.

There's a _____ and a _____.

There are _____ and there are _____. I like my town! 🙂

Love, _____.

My town

3 Play *The Town Game.* See TG notes.

There's a post office. There are lots of clothes shops.
a bookshop, a police station, a cafe, a playground, a toy shop, a school, a post office, a clothes shop

p 92

11

1 Lesson 7 Sound play

1 Listen and point. Repeat. 🔊 1.15–1.16

A B C D E F G H I J K L M N O P Q R S T U V W X Y Z

2 Sing *The Alphabet Song*. 🔊 1.17–1.18

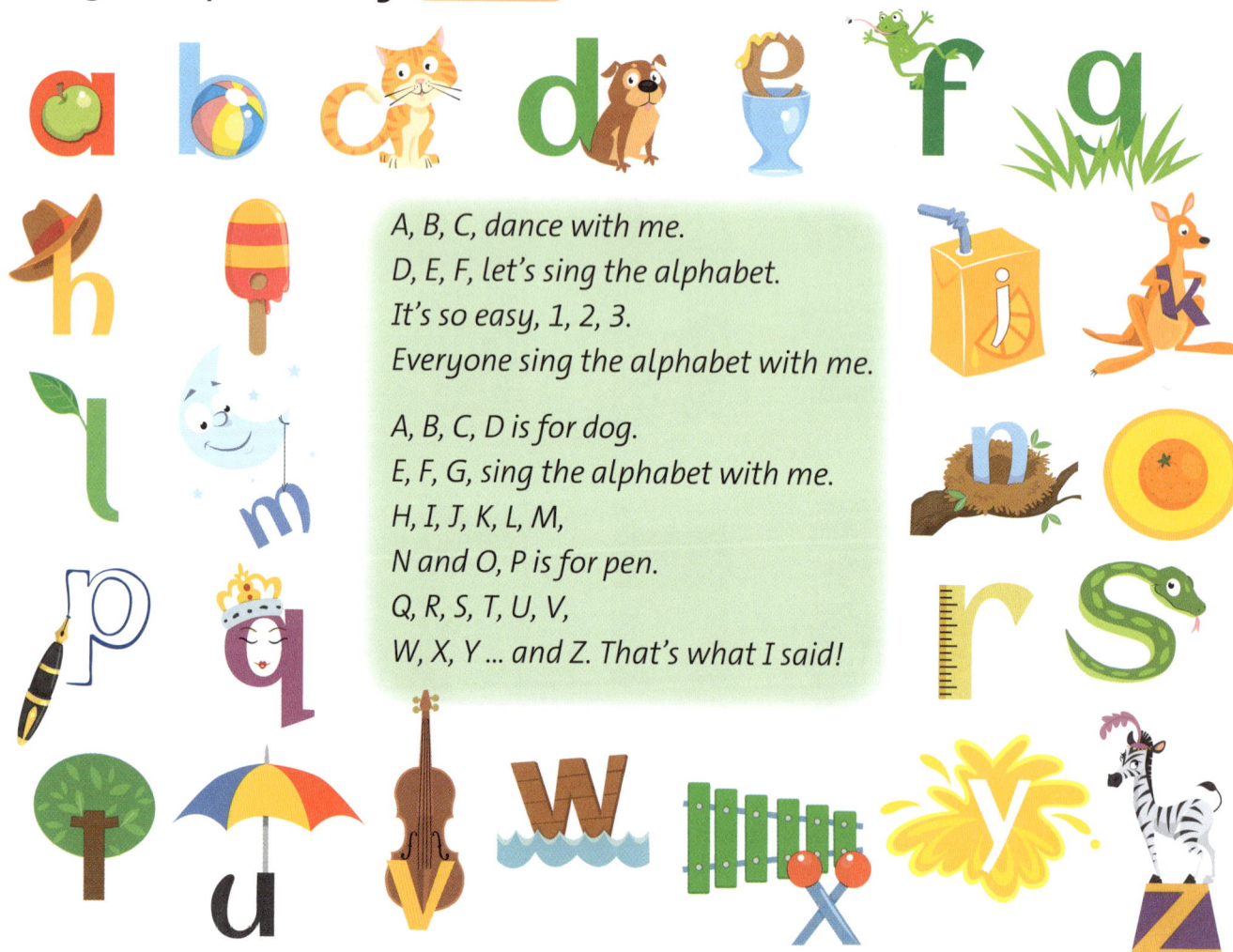

A, B, C, dance with me.
D, E, F, let's sing the alphabet.
It's so easy, 1, 2, 3.
Everyone sing the alphabet with me.

A, B, C, D is for dog.
E, F, G, sing the alphabet with me.
H, I, J, K, L, M,
N and O, P is for pen.
Q, R, S, T, U, V,
W, X, Y … and Z. That's what I said!

3 Listen and colour. Then say. 🔊 1.19

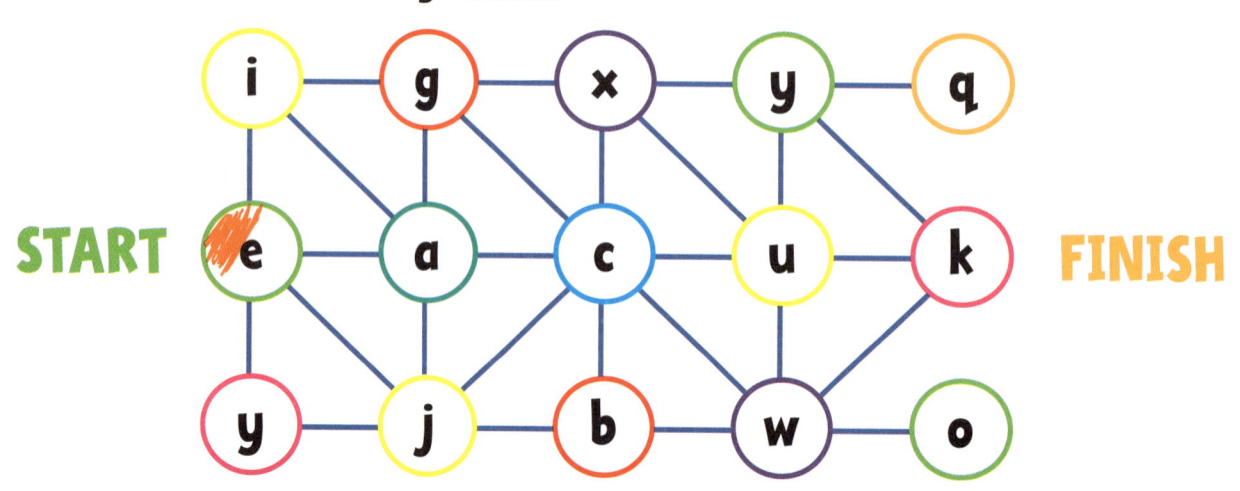

START … FINISH

4 Draw the alphabet. *See TG notes.*

The alphabet

Lesson 8 Round up

1 Listen and number. Then write and say. 🔊 1.20

1 _____
2 _____
3 _____
4 _____
5 _____

2 Circle and write.

1 **There's / There are** a _____.
2 **There's / There are** lots of _____.
3 **There's / There are** a _____.
4 **There's / There are** two _____.

3 🏠 **Take Home English** Make *My town.* See TG notes.

This is my town. There's a school. There are lots of trees.

There's a school. There are three bikes. There are lots of leaves.
a bookshop, a police station, a cafe, a playground, a toy shop, a school, a post office, a clothes shop

13

2 Numbers — Lesson 1

1 Listen and point. Repeat. Listen and colour. 🔊 1.21–1.23

2 **Think** Talk about numbers. *See TG notes.*

○ eleven ✓ twelve ○ thirteen ○ fourteen ○ fifteen
○ sixteen ○ seventeen ○ eighteen ○ nineteen ○ twenty

3 Chant. 🔊 1.24

4 Play *Three in a Row.* *See TG notes.*

14   eleven, twelve, thirteen, fourteen, fifteen, sixteen, seventeen, eighteen, nineteen, twenty   p 93

Lesson 2

1 Write and say.

2 Sing *The Raft Race Song*. 🔊 1.25–1.26

There are ten people in the raft race today,
Ten people in the raft race today.
Let's count the people in the raft race today.
Are you ready? Hip, hip, hooray!

One, two, three,
Four, five, six,
Seven, eight, nine, ten people!
Hip, hip, hooray!
Let's find more people for the raft race today.

Eleven, twelve, thirteen,
Fourteen, fifteen, sixteen,
Seventeen, eighteen, nineteen, twenty people!
Hip, hip, hooray!
There are twenty people in the raft race today!

---

eleven, twelve, thirteen, fourteen, fifteen, sixteen, seventeen, eighteen, nineteen, twenty

2 Lesson 3 Catch!

1 **Think** Listen. Where's the story? 🔊 1.27 *See TG notes.*

2 Now watch or listen and read. ▶ 🔊 1.28

1 What's your name? / My name's Russ.

2 Hi, Russ. How old are you? / I'm eight.

3 Where are you from? / I'm from Bridge Town.

4 Look, Emily. It's the boat! / No, it isn't. It's number 18!

5 *Along the canal ...* Look!

6 It's Sniff! Come on, Sniff!

It's the boat. No, it isn't. It's number 18! Come on, Sniff! Catch!

Lesson 4

7 Sniff, catch!

8 Oh no, Sniff! MEOW!
Sniff? Who's Sniff?

1 Look and tick (✓).

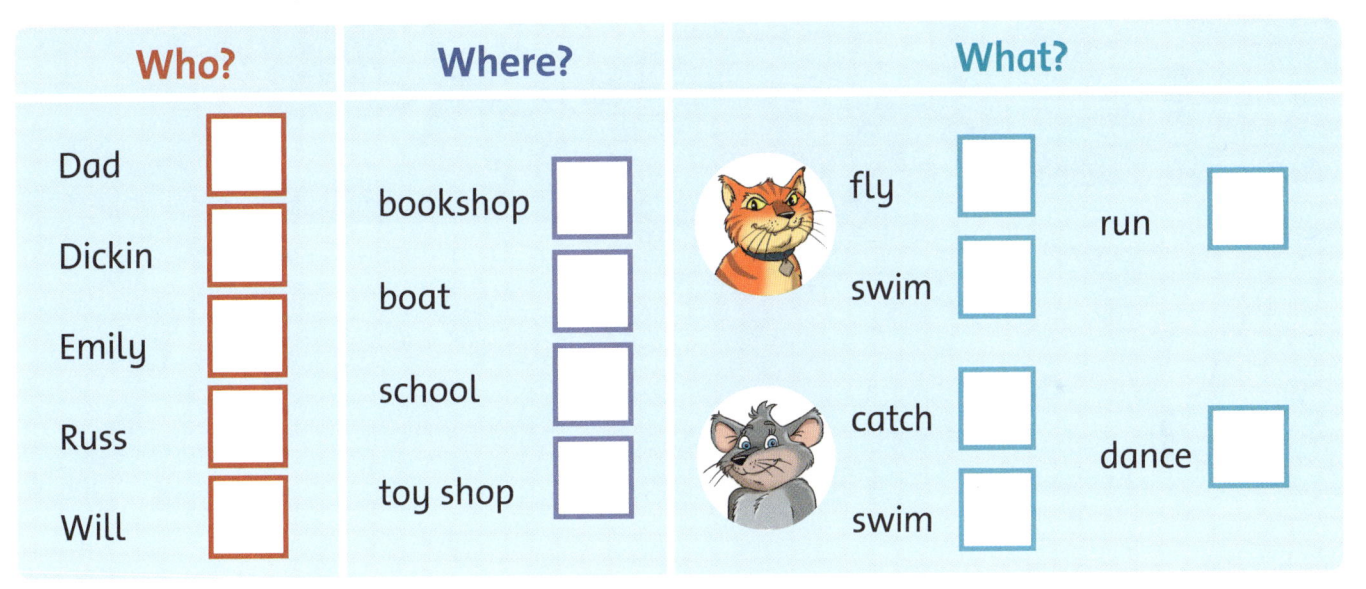

Who?	Where?	What?	
Dad	bookshop	fly	run
Dickin	boat	swim	
Emily	school	catch	dance
Russ	toy shop	swim	
Will			

2 Who makes a new friend? Look and tick (✓).

3 Think Talk about making friends. *See TG notes.*

p 94

17

Lesson 5

1 Listen and repeat. Then ask and answer. 🔊 1.29

> What's your name?
> How old are you?
> Where are you from?
>
> My name's Emily.
> I'm 6.
> I'm from Bridge Town.

2 Write.

1 _____? I'm from Bridge Town.
2 _____? My name's Fern.
3 _____? I'm eight.

3 Answer for you.

1 What's your name? _____.
2 How old are you? _____.
3 Where are you from? _____.

18 What's your name? My name's … How old are you? I'm …
Where are you from? I'm from …

Grammar p 115   p 95

Lesson 6 **2**

1 Listen and tick (✓). 🔊 1.30

1 What's your name?
   Marco ☐   Patty ☐   Tom ☐

2 How old are you?
   8 ☐   9 ☐   11 ☐

3 Where are you from?
   Rome ☐   New York ☐   London ☐

2 Write a letter.

| from   name   nine   playgrounds   post office   What   Where   you |

16 Clinton Street
New York

Hello!

My _____'s Patty. I'm _____ New York.

I'm 9 _____. _____'s your name?

How old are _____? _____ are you from?

In my town, there's a 🏪 _____ and there are

lots of 🛝 _____. What's in your town?

Love, Patty.

This is me.

3 Play *The Chain Game.* See TG notes.

What's your name? My name's … How old are you? I'm … Where are you from? I'm from …
eleven, twelve, thirteen, fourteen, fifteen, sixteen, seventeen, eighteen, nineteen, twenty

p 95   19

Lesson 7 Sound play

1 Listen and repeat. Can you hear the sound? 🔊 1.31

cake   play   rain

2 Listen and tick (✓) if you hear the sound. 🔊 1.32

game ☐   eight ☐   apple ☐   paint ☐   name ☐

3 Listen and check. Repeat. 🔊 1.33

4 Listen and say. 🔊 1.34

Eight cakes play a game in the rain.

cake, play, rain, game, eight, paint, name

Lesson 8 Round up

1 Listen and write. Then write the words. 🔊 1.35

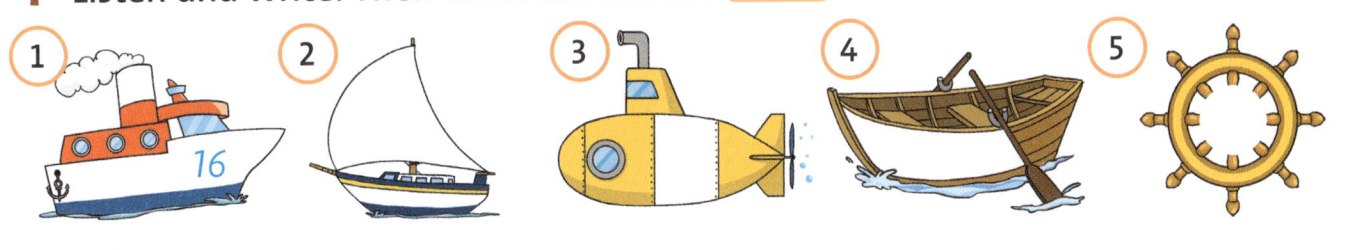

1. 16 — sixteen
2. ___
3. ___
4. ___
5. ___
6. ___
7. ___
8. ___
9. ___
10. ___

2 Put the words in order. Then answer the questions.

1. name   your   What's   _____?
   _____.

2. are   How   you   old   _____?
   _____.

3. you   are   from   Where   _____?
   _____.

3 🏠 **Take Home English** Make a *This is me* lapbook. *See TG notes.*

What's your name?
Where are you from?
How old are you?

My name's Anna.
I'm from Bristol.
I'm nine.

What's your name? My name's ... How old are you? I'm ... Where are you from? I'm from ...
eleven, twelve, thirteen, fourteen, fifteen, sixteen, seventeen, eighteen, nineteen, twenty

21

At the station

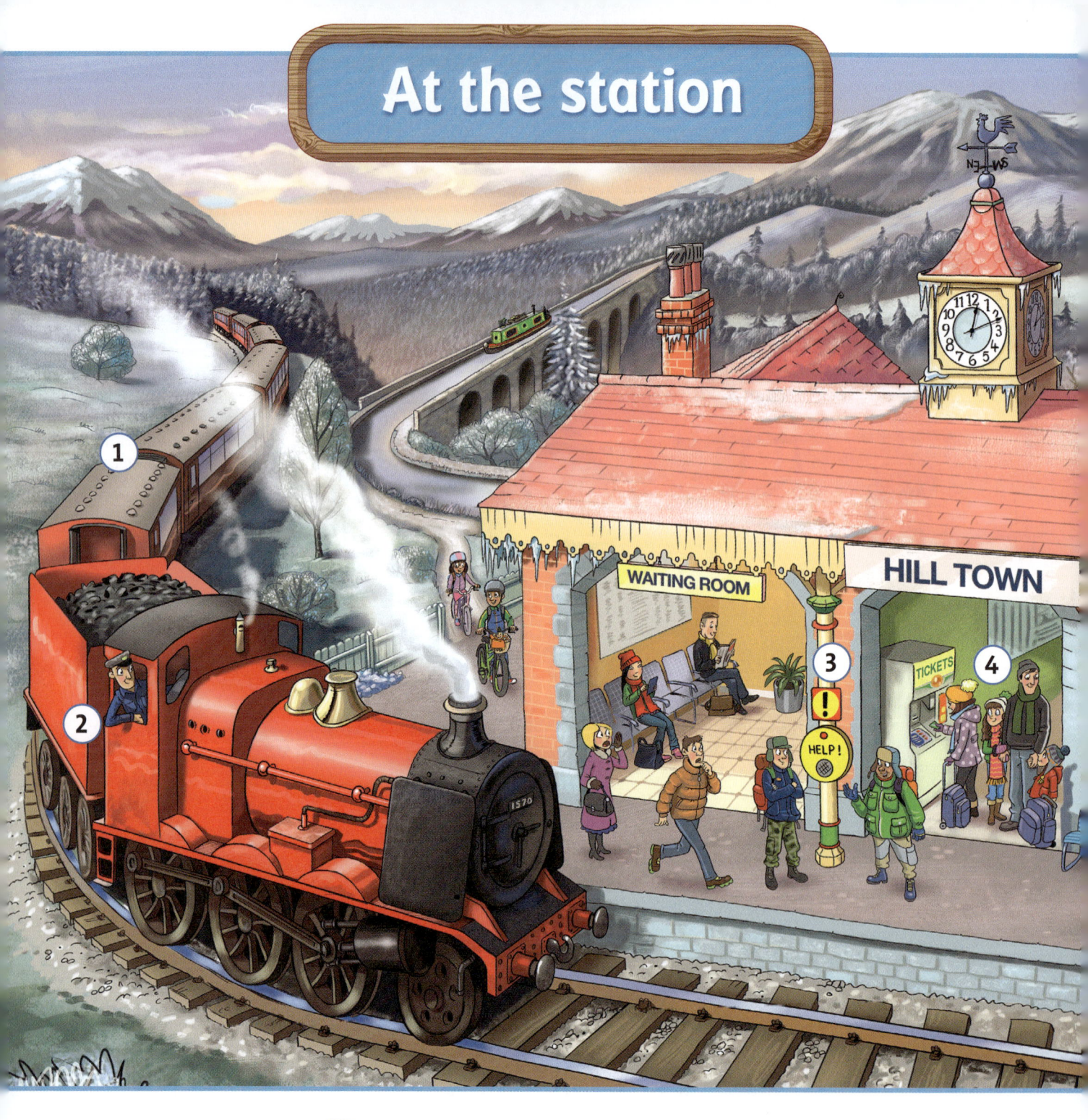

1 Watch the video. ▶

2 (Think) Talk about transport. *See TG notes.*

3 Listen and point. Repeat. Write. 🔊 1.36–1.37

> passengers   icicles   a help point
> a train driver   a train   a police officer

1 _____   2 _____   3 _____

4 _____   5 _____   6 _____

22

Units **3–4**
Citizenship

4 Sing *The Keep Safe! Song.* 🔊 1.38–1.39

*Keep safe at the station, everyone.
Hold hands with Dad and Mum.
Don't get lost. Don't run off.
Keep safe when the passengers come and go.*

*When you can't find Mum
And you can't find Dad.*

*Ask for help. It's OK.
Keep safe and enjoy your day!*

*Look! A police officer. Say hi.
Look! A train driver. Wave goodbye.
Look! Icicles and snow.
We're on the train. Off we go!*

5 Class project Make a Keep Safe! poster. See TG notes.

6 The story so far Listen and answer the questions. 🔊 1.40 See TG notes.

passengers, icicles, a help point, a train driver, a train, a police officer
Keep safe. Hold hands. Ask for help.

🎵 p124

23

3 Food and drink — Lesson 1

1 Listen and point. Repeat. Number. 🔊 1.41–1.42

2 **Think** Talk about food and drink. *See TG notes.*

STATION CAFE

☐ spaghetti ☐ salad ☐ rice ☐ fish
☐ milk ☐ bread ☐ chicken ☐ soup

3 Chant. 🔊 1.43

4 Play *The Letters Game. See TG notes.*

24   spaghetti, salad, rice, fish, milk, bread, chicken, soup

p 96

Lesson 2

1 Write and say.

2 Sing *The Food Song*. 🔊 1.44–1.45

My favourite food is spaghetti and grapes.
But I really love rice and cakes.
When the waiter comes, I just can't wait
To eat my favourite food, spaghetti and grapes.

Waiter, waiter! Excuse me, please.
I don't like bread. I don't like cheese.
I like salad and lemonade, too.
But spaghetti and grapes are my favourite foods.
Yes, OK. I've got that for you.

Waiter, waiter! Excuse me, please.
I don't like soup. I don't like cheese.
I like sandwiches and fish, too.
But spaghetti and grapes are my favourite foods.
Yes, OK. I've got that for you.

spaghetti, salad, rice, fish, milk, bread, chicken, soup

Lesson 3 I'm hungry!

1 Think Listen. Where's the story? 🔊 1.46 *See TG notes.*

2 Now watch or listen and read. ▶ 🔊 1.47

1 Where's Will? / It's OK, Fern.

2 I'm hungry. / I'm thirsty. / Look! There's a cafe.

3 Menu / Do you like soup, Fern? / No, I don't like soup.

4 Do you like salad? / Yes, I like salad. / I don't like fish!

5 Menu / Hello, everyone! / Will!

6 I'm very happy, Will. / And I'm hungry!

Where's Will? I'm hungry. I'm thirsty. This is Emily. Sorry. No, thank you.

Lesson 4

3

I've got sandwiches and juice.	Orange juice, Rowan?
This is Emily.	Yuck!
And Russ!	Sorry. No, thank you, Will.
	Rowan!

1 Read and match. Write the story frame number.

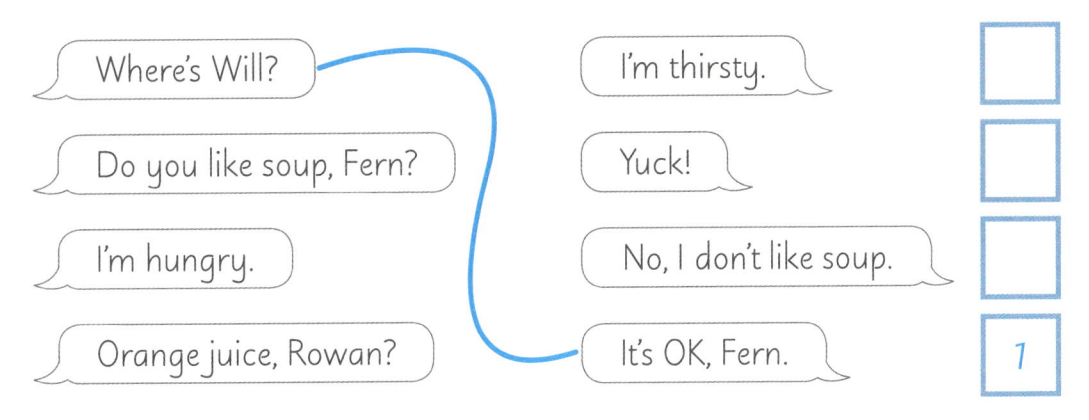

- Where's Will? — It's OK, Fern. → 1
- Do you like soup, Fern? — No, I don't like soup.
- I'm hungry. — I'm thirsty.
- Orange juice, Rowan? — Yuck!

2 Which pictures show Rowan being polite? Look and tick (✓).

- Yes, please.
- Yuck!
- No, thank you.

3 Think — Talk about being polite. *See TG notes.*

p 97

27

3 Lesson 5

1 Listen and repeat. Then ask and answer. 🔊 1.48

Do you like spaghetti?

Do you like rice?

Menu
spaghetti
chicken
milk
rice
salad

Yes, I like spaghetti.

No, I don't like rice.

2 Write.

1. Do you __like__ milk?   __No__, I __don't__ __like__ milk.
2. Do _____ _____ rice?   Yes, I _____ rice.
3. _____ _____ _____ soup?   _____, I _____ soup.
4. _____ _____ _____ fish?   _____, I _____ _____ fish.

3 Answer for you. Then ask a friend.

1. Do you like fish?   _____, _____.
2. Do you like spaghetti?   _____, _____.
3. Do you like bread?   _____, _____.
4. Do you like chicken?   _____, _____.

Do you like spaghetti? Yes, I like spaghetti. No, I don't like spaghetti.

Grammar p 116   p 98

Lesson 6

3

1 Listen and tick (✓) or cross (✗). 🔊 1.49

Do you like bread?

Yes, I like bread.

Ben   Amy

2 Ask and answer. Tick (✓) or cross (✗).

Me					
My friend					

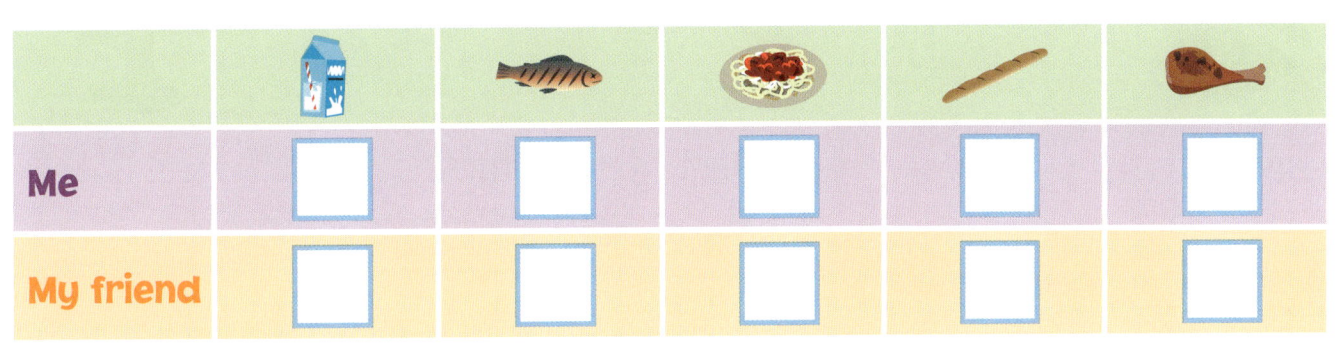

3 Draw and write.

MENU

I like _____.
I _____.
I don't like _____.
I _____.

4 Play *The Food Game.* See TG notes.

Do you like bread? Yes, I like bread. No, I don't like bread.
spaghetti, salad, rice, fish, milk, bread, chicken, soup

p 98

29

3 Lesson 7 Sound play

1 Listen and repeat. Can you hear the sound? 🔊 1.50

bee   tea   cheese

2 Listen and tick (✓) if you hear the sound. 🔊 1.51

leaves ☐   fish ☐   feet ☐   three ☐   tree ☐

3 Listen and check. Repeat. 🔊 1.52

4 Listen and say. 🔊 1.53

Three bees eat cheese in a tree.

bee, tea, cheese, leaves, feet, three, tree

Lesson 8 Round up 3

1 Listen and number. Then write and say. 🔊 1.54

2 Look and write.

1. 🥛 Do you _____ ? 🙂 Yes , _____ .
2. 🍚 _____ ? ☹️ _____ , _____ .
3. 🍲 _____ ? ☹️ _____ , _____ .
4. 🐟 _____ ? 🙂 _____ , _____ .

3 🏠 **Take Home English** Make a *My food and drink* book. *See TG notes.*

Do you like salad?
Yes, I like salad.

Do you like rice? Yes, I like rice. No, I don't like rice.
spaghetti, salad, rice, fish, milk, bread, chicken, soup

31

4 At the shop — Lesson 1

1 Listen and point. Repeat. Write. 2.1–2.2

2 **Think** Talk about shopping. *See TG notes.*

STATION GIFTS

a key ring   an ice cream   a car   a doll   a comic
a ball   a postcard   a puzzle

3 Chant. 2.3

4 Play *The Guessing Game*. *See TG notes.*

a key ring, an ice cream, a car, a doll, a comic, a ball, a postcard, a puzzle

p 99

Lesson 2

1 Listen and point. Repeat. Write. 2.4–2.5

twenty   forty   ten   one hundred   sixty   thirty
seventy   fifty   ninety   eighty

1. 10 _____
2. 20 _____
3. 30 _____
4. 40 _____
5. 50 _____

6. 60 _____
7. 70 _____
8. 80 _____
9. 90 _____
10. 100 _____

2 Sing *The Shopping Song*. 2.6–2.7

We're at the market, at the market.
We love shopping at the market.
At the market, at the market.
What do you like at the market?

A key ring, please. A key ring, please.
Ten cents for a key ring, please.
An ice cream, please. An ice cream, please.
Twenty cents for an ice cream, please.
A postcard, please. A postcard, please.
Thirty cents for a postcard, please.

ten, twenty, thirty, forty, fifty, sixty, seventy, eighty, ninety, one hundred

4 Lesson 3 Look! It's a doll

1 **Think** Listen. Where's the story? 2.8 See TG notes.

2 Now watch or listen and read. 2.9

1
— I like ice cream.
— Ice cream? But … it's cold!

2
— I've got an idea. Wait here!

3
— Can I have an ice cream, please?
— Yes, here you are.

4
— How much is it?
— It's 80 cents.
— Poppy, come back!

5
— Mum, look! It's a doll.
— Come on, Anna! The train.

6
— Oh no, Poppy!
— Help me!

It's cold. I've got an idea. Wait here! Help me! It's a doll. Here's the ice cream!

34

Lesson 4

7 Quick!

8 Here's the ice cream! Will, look!

1 Look and tick (✓). Match.

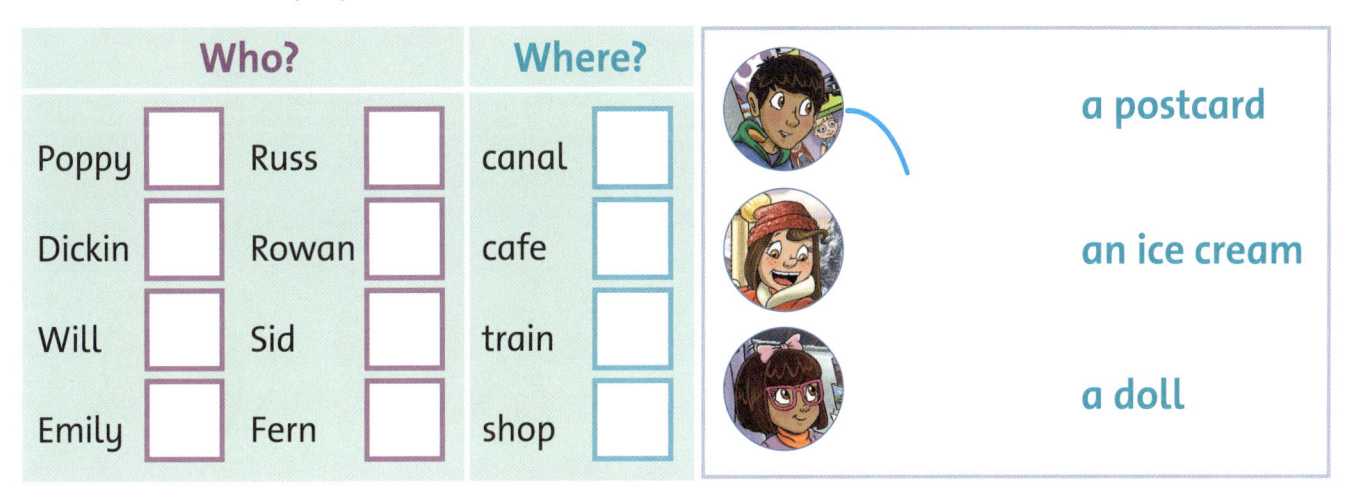

Who?		Where?	
Poppy ☐	Russ ☐	canal ☐	
Dickin ☐	Rowan ☐	cafe ☐	
Will ☐	Sid ☐	train ☐	
Emily ☐	Fern ☐	shop ☐	

a postcard

an ice cream

a doll

2 Who follows instructions? Look and tick (✓).

3 (Think) Talk about following instructions. *See TG notes.*

p 100

35

4 Lesson 5

1 Listen and repeat. Then ask and answer. 🔊 2.10

> Can I have a postcard, please?
> How much is it?
> Yes, here you are.
> It's 20 cents.

2 Count and write.

~~forty~~   sixty   seventy   eighty

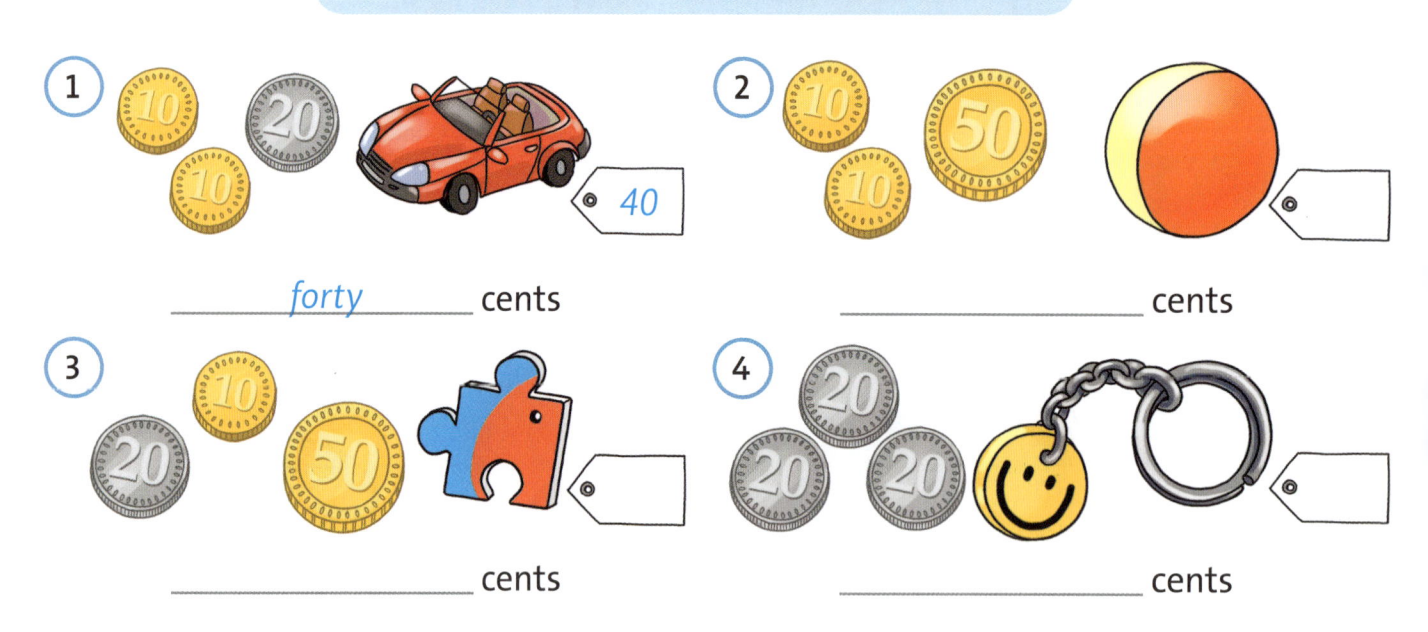

1. ____forty____ cents
2. _____ cents
3. _____ cents
4. _____ cents

3 Write. Then ask and answer.

1 Can I have ____a car____, please? Yes, ____here____ you are.
2 How much _____ _____? It's forty cents.
3 _____ I have _____, please? Yes, _____ you are.
4 _____ _____ is it? It's _____ cents.

Can I have a postcard, please? Yes, here you are. How much is it? It's 20 cents.

Grammar p 117   p 101

Lesson 6

1 Listen, match and circle. 🔊 2.11

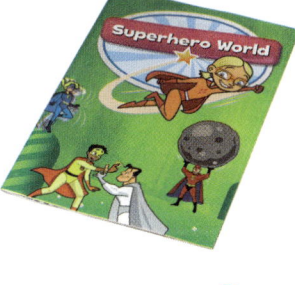

2 Draw and write.

Can I have _____, please?

Yes, _____ _____ _____.

How _____ _____ _____?

_____ _____ cents.

3 Play *The Shopping Game.* See TG notes.

Can I have a comic, please? Yes, here you are. How much is it? It's fifty cents.
a key ring, an ice cream, a car, a doll, a comic, a ball, a postcard, a puzzle
ten, twenty, thirty, forty, fifty, sixty, seventy, eighty, ninety, one hundred

p 101

37

4 Lesson 7 Sound play

1 Listen and repeat. Can you hear the sound? 🔊 2.12

five

fly

white

2 Listen and tick (✓) if you hear the sound. 🔊 2.13

rice ☐ bike ☐ climb ☐ winter ☐ ice ☐

3 Listen and check. Repeat. 🔊 2.14

4 Listen and say. 🔊 2.15

I like white rice and my bike made of ice.

five, fly, white, rice, bike, climb, ice

Lesson 8 Round up

1 Listen and write the numbers. Then write and say. 🔊 2.16

_____ key ring _____

2 Write and number.

☐ _____, here _____ are.

☐ It's 20 20 _____ cents.

1 _____ Can _____ I _____ _____, please?

☐ How much _____ _____ ?

3 🏠 **Take Home English** Make *My shop*. See TG notes.

Can I have a key ring, please?
Yes, here you are.
How much is it?
It's thirty cents.

Can I have a key ring, please? Yes, here you are. How much is it? It's 40 cents.
a key ring, an ice cream, a car, a doll, a comic, a ball, a postcard, a puzzle
ten, twenty, thirty, forty, fifty, sixty, seventy, eighty, ninety, one hundred

39

In the woods

1 Watch the video.

2 **Think** Talk about nature. *See TG notes.*

3 Listen and point. Repeat. Write. 2.17–2.18

> litter   a bin   a plastic bag
> a sign   a bottle   a can

1 _____   2 _____   3 _____

4 _____   5 _____   6 _____

40

Units 5–6
Environmental education

4 Sing *The Clean Up! Song*. 2.19–2.20

Let's go for a walk in Bluebell Woods.
Don't drop litter, it's not good!
There are blue flowers and lots of trees.
There are birds hiding in the leaves!
Let's help the animals, keep the woods clean.
Look at the signs, and work as a team.

Pick up your bottle, and put it in the bin.
Pick up your bag, and put it in the bin.
Pick up your can, and put it in the bin.

Don't drop litter, it's not good.
Don't drop litter in Bluebell Woods!

5 Class project Make a Clean Up! poster. *See TG notes.*

6 The story so far Listen and answer the questions. 2.21 *See TG notes.*

litter, a bin, a plastic bag, a sign, a bottle, a can
Don't drop litter. Pick up your bottle. Put it in the bin.

5 My bedroom — Lesson 1

1 Listen and point. Repeat. Write. 🔊 2.22–2.23

2 Think Talk about your bedroom. *See TG notes.*

a desk   a bed   a bookshelf   a lamp   a rug
a wardrobe   a chair   drawers

3 Chant. 🔊 2.24

4 Play *I Spy*. *See TG notes.*

42   a desk, a bed, a bookshelf, a lamp, a rug, a wardrobe, a chair, drawers   p102

Lesson 2

5

1 Write about picture A.

1 There's a blue ____bed____ and there are two yellow _____.
2 There are two white _____ and there are two red _____.
3 There's an orange _____ and there are purple _____.
4 There's a brown _____ and there are two green _____.

2 What's different in picture B? Say.

> In picture B, there's a …

3 Sing the *I Love My Bedroom Song*. 2.25–2.26

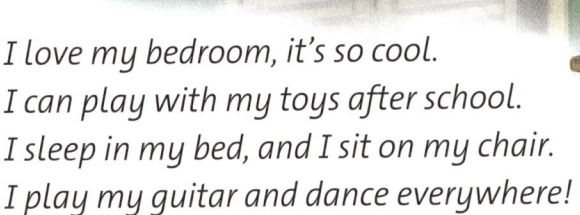

I love my bedroom, it's so cool.
I can play with my toys after school.
I sleep in my bed, and I sit on my chair.
I play my guitar and dance everywhere!

There's a desk in my room.
It's so cool there's a desk in my room.
I've got a lamp in my room.
It's so cool I've got a lamp in my room.
I've got a wardrobe in my room.
Oh yeah, oh yeah.

There's a blue bed and there are two yellow bookshelves.
a desk, a bed, a bookshelf, a lamp, a rug, a wardrobe, a chair, drawers

p 124   p 102

5 Lesson 3 We're lost!

1 **Think** Listen. Where's the story? 🔊 2.27 See TG notes.

2 Now watch or listen and read. ▶ 🔊 2.28

1 There are beds in the train! And there's Poppy! Shh!

2 I'm so happy! Oh no! Bridge Town is the other way!

3 Next station, Bluebell Woods. Come on! Follow me.

4 There's a red traffic light. Let's go!

5 Whee!

6 Hello! Aargh!

7 It's OK. I'm your friend. I'm Sam. Hello, Sam. Please help us. We're lost.

Bridge Town is the other way! I'm your friend. Please help us. We're lost. Let's send a message!

Lesson 4

5

8 Come with me.

9 There's a phone on the desk. Let's send a message!

10 Will, where are you? From Russ
I'm in Sea Town! From Will

1 Read and tick (✓). Then say.

		Yes	No
1	I'm so happy!	✓	
2	There's a green traffic light.		
3	I'm your friend. I'm Sam.		
4	I'm in Bridge Town.		

2 Who helps others? Look and tick (✓).

3 **Think** Talk about helping others. *See TG notes.*

p 103

45

5 Lesson 5

1 Listen and write. Repeat. 🔊 2.29–2.30

in   on   under

2 Look at the picture in activity 1. Read and circle.

1 There's a phone **in** / **(on)** / **under** the desk.

2 There are books **in** / **on** / **under** the wardrobe.

3 There are cars **in** / **on** / **under** the bookshelf.

4 There's a ball **in** / **on** / **under** the bed.

5 There's a comic **in** / **on** / **under** the bag.

3 Look, circle and write.

1 **There's** / **(There are)** three key rings ____on____ the desk.

2 **There's** / **There are** a puzzle _____ the bed.

3 **There's** / **There are** two dolls _____ the chair.

4 **There's** / **There are** a bag _____ the wardrobe.

There's a phone in / on / under the desk.
There are books in / on / under the wardrobe.

Grammar p 118   p 104

Lesson 6

1 Listen and number. Then say. 🔊 2.31

1 2 3 4

2 Draw and write. Then colour.

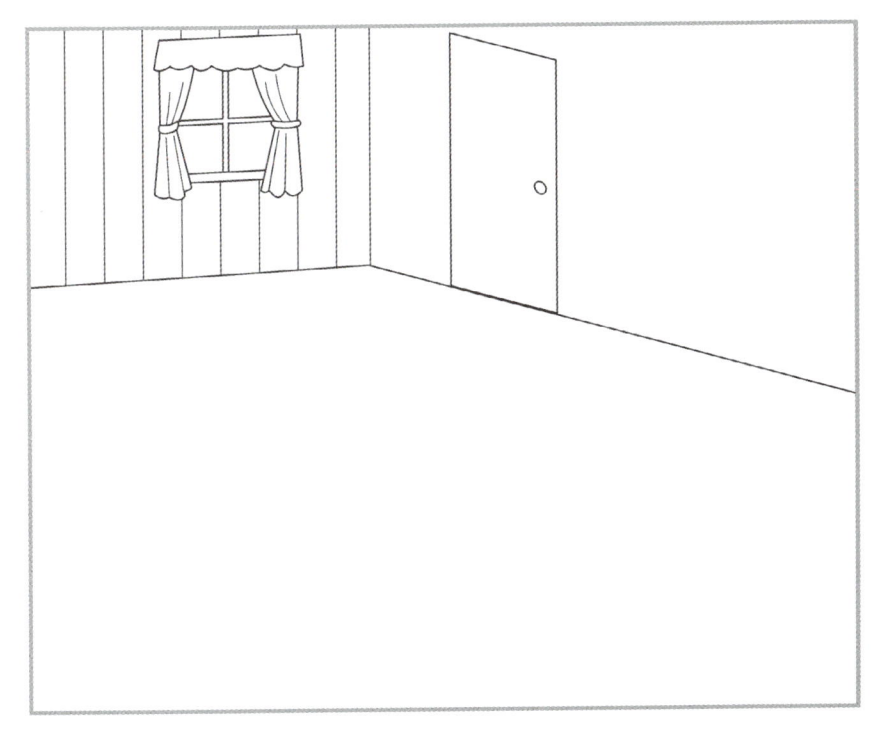

1 There's a _____ in the _____.

2 There are two red _____ on the _____.

3 There's a blue _____ under the _____.

4 There's a _____ on the _____.

3 Play *The Guessing Game.* See TG notes.

There's a doll in / on / under the bed. There are books in / on / under the chair.
a desk, a bed, a bookshelf, a lamp, a rug, a wardrobe, a chair, drawers

p 104

47

5 Lesson 7 Sound play

1 Listen and repeat. Can you hear the sound? 🔊 2.32

bedroom

blue

shoe

2 Listen and tick (✓) if you hear the sound. 🔊 2.33

soup  ☐   boot  ☐   food 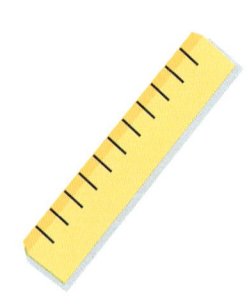 ☐   ruler  ☐   robot ☐

3 Listen and check. Repeat. 🔊 2.34

4 Listen and say. 🔊 2.35

There are shoes and boots in her blue bedroom.

bedroom, blue, shoe, soup, boot, food, ruler

48

Lesson 8 **Round up** 5

1 Listen and number. Then write. 🔊 2.36

1 _____
2 _____
3 _____
4 _____
5 _____
6 _____
7 _____

2 Look at the picture in activity 1 and write.

1 ___*There's*___ a lamp _____ the desk.
2 _____ a teddy _____ the drawers.
3 _____ three books _____ the bookshelf.
4 _____ a ball _____ the wardrobe.

There's
There are
in
on
under

3 🏠 **Take Home English** Make *My bedroom*. See TG notes.

This is my bedroom. There's a bed and a wardrobe.

There's a T-shirt in the wardrobe.

There's a lamp in / on / under the bed. There are three books in / on / under the chair.
a desk, a bed, a bookshelf, a lamp, a rug, a wardrobe, a chair, drawers

49

6 Playtime — Lesson 1

1 Listen and point. Repeat. Write. 🔊 2.37–2.38

2 Think Talk about your favourite things. See TG notes.

a racket   a bike   a poster   a helmet   a tablet
a Frisbee   a skateboard   a kite

3 Chant. 🔊 2.39

4 Play *The Miming Game.* See TG notes.

a racket, a bike, a poster, a helmet, a tablet, a Frisbee, a skateboard, a kite

p 105

Lesson 2

6

1 Look and write. Then say.

1. I've got a _____ and a _____.
2. I've got a _____ and a _____.
3. I've got a _____ and a _____.
4. I've got a _____ and a _____.

2 Sing *The Playtime Song*. 2.40–2.41

Hey, everyone. It's sunny today.
Let's go outdoors, have fun and play.
We can play with a bike, or jump and run.
Let's find some toys and have some fun!

Where's my racket? It's under the bed.
Where's my poster? It's on the door.
Where's my kite? It's in the garden.
Hooray, hooray. Let's play with my kite today!

Where's my tablet? It's on the chair.
Where's my skateboard? It's in the hall.
Where's my Frisbee? It's under the desk.
Hooray, hooray. Let's play with my Frisbee today!

I've got a poster and a tablet.
a racket, a bike, a poster, a helmet, a tablet, a Frisbee, a skateboard, a kite

p 105

51

6 Lesson 3 Don't wake Buddy!

1 Think Listen. Where's the story? 🔊 2.42 *See TG notes.*

2 Now watch or listen and read. ▶ 🔊 2.43

1 I've got an idea. Come with me.

2 Let's take the skateboard.

3 Look! He's got a kite.

4 Shh! Don't wake Buddy!

5 Ready, steady, go!

6 Whee … Oh no! Humans!

Let's take the skateboard. Don't wake Buddy! Ready, steady, go! Humans!

Lesson 4 6

7 SCREECH!

8 Quick! Run!

9 Now she's got the skateboard!
And he's got the kite!

1 Look and tick (✓). Draw what happens next.

Who?		Where?
Sniff ☐	Fern ☐	Bridge Town ☐
Dickin ☐	Rowan ☐	Hill Town ☐
Sid ☐	Poppy ☐	Bluebell Woods ☐
Emily ☐	Russ ☐	Sea Town ☐
Will ☐	Sam ☐	

2 Which picture shows teamwork? Look and tick (✓).

3 (Think) Talk about teamwork. *See TG notes.*

p 106   53

6 Lesson 5

1 Listen and repeat. Then say. 2.44

She's got a kite.

He's got a Frisbee.

2 Look at the picture in activity 1 and write.

1 _____ a Frisbee.   4 _____ a kite.

2 _____ a tablet.   5 _____ a skateboard.

3 _____ a helmet.   6 _____ a racket.

3 Look and write. Say.

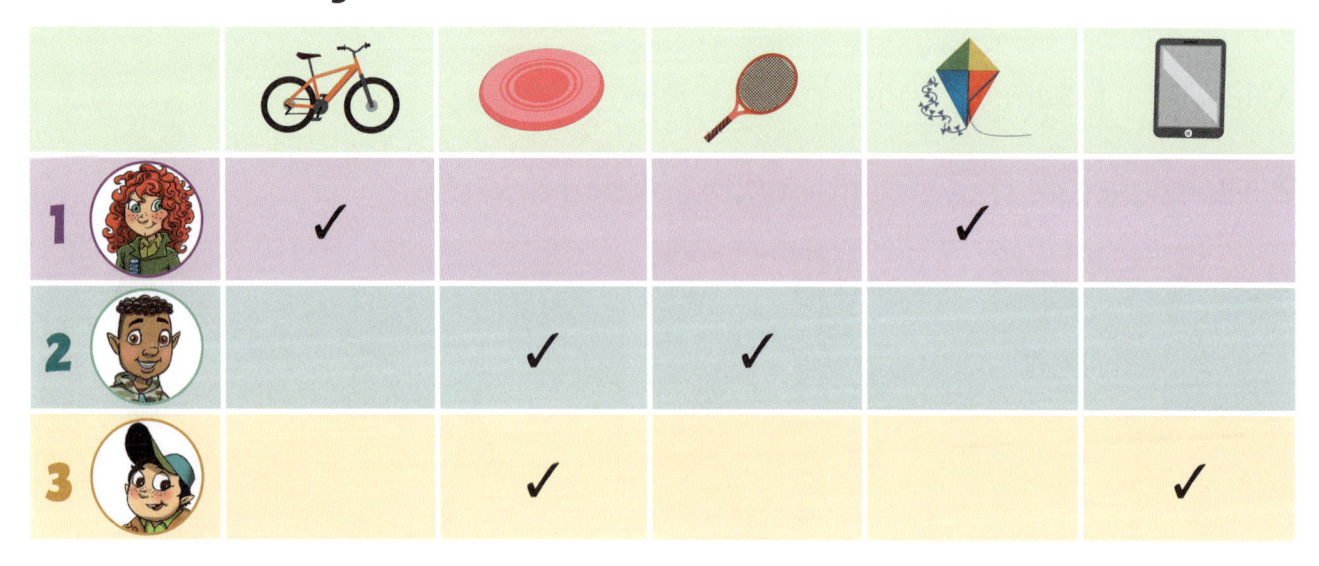

1 _____ a bike and a _____.

2 _____ a _____ and a racket.

3 _____ a _____ and a _____.

She's got a kite. He's got a Frisbee.

Grammar p 119   p 107

54

Lesson 6

1 Listen and tick (✓). Then say. 🔊 2.45

2 Draw and write. Then say.

3 — Me

_____   _____   I'_____
a _____ and   a _____ and   a _____ and
a _____ .   a _____ .   a _____ .

3 Play *Guess What?* *See TG notes.*

She's got a tablet. He's got a poster. I've got a bike.
a racket, a bike, a poster, a helmet, a tablet, a Frisbee, a skateboard, a kite

p 107

55

6 Lesson 7 Sound play

1 Listen and repeat. Can you hear the sound? 🔊 2.46

hello   boat   go

2 Listen and tick (✓) if you hear the sound. 🔊 2.47

socks ☐   postcard ☐   nose ☐   wardrobe ☐   coat ☐

3 Listen and check. Repeat. 🔊 2.48

4 Listen and say. 🔊 2.49

Hello!

He's got a wardrobe and a coat in his yellow boat.

hello, boat, go, postcard, nose, wardrobe, coat

Lesson 8 Round up 6

1 Listen and number. Then write and say. 🔊 2.50

2 Look and write.   He's got   She's got

1. _____ a 🛹 _____ and a 🥏 _____.
2. _____ a 🎬 _____ and a 📱 _____.
3. _____ a 🎾 _____ and a ⛑️ _____.
4. _____ a 🪁 _____ and a 🚲 _____.

3 🏠 **Take Home English** Make a *My favourite things* lapbook. *See TG notes.*

"I've got a skateboard and a tablet."

She's got a skateboard and a kite. He's got a racket and a Frisbee.
a racket, a bike, a poster, a helmet, a tablet, a Frisbee, a skateboard, a kite

57

At the beach

1 Watch the video.

2 **Think** Talk about the summer holidays. *See TG notes.*

3 Listen and point. Repeat. Write. 2.51–2.52

> a whistle   goggles   a towel
> the sea   a flag   a lifeguard

1 _____   2 _____   3 _____

4 _____   5 _____   6 _____

58

Units
Health and safety
7–8

4 Sing the *Respect the Rules Song*. 🔊 2.53–2.54

Let's swim, let's run, let's have fun.
Respect the rules in the summer sun.
Come on, everyone, let's have fun.
Respect the rules in the summer sun.

Look, there's a lifeguard, can you see?
He's got a whistle ... 1, 2, 3.
Look, there's a red flag, can you see?
I can't swim today in the sea.

5 Class project Make a Rules poster. *See TG notes.*

6 The story so far Listen and answer the questions. 🔊 2.55 *See TG notes.*

a whistle, goggles, a towel, the sea, a flag, a lifeguard
There's a red flag. I can't swim today. I can swim.

🎵 p124

59

7 Clothes — Lesson 1

1 Listen and point. Repeat. Write. 🔊 2.56–2.57

2 **Think** Talk about your clothes. See TG notes.

a tracksuit   shorts   trainers   sandals
a skirt   a T-shirt   a dress   trousers

3 Chant. 🔊 2.58

4 Play *The Memory Game.* See TG notes.

a tracksuit, shorts, trainers, sandals, a skirt, a T-shirt, a dress, trousers

p108

Lesson 2

7

1 Look and write. Then say.

He's got blue _____,
a red _____ and green
_____. He's got orange
_____, too.

She's got a purple _____,
red _____ and a black
and white _____. She's
got a blue _____, too.

2 Sing *The Fashion Song.* 2.59–2.60

*There's a fashion show, a fashion show.
Let's all go to the fashion show.
What colour are your favourite clothes?
Let's find out at the fashion show!*

*He's got a blue tracksuit,
A blue, blue, blue tracksuit.
He's got red shorts,
Red, red, red shorts.
He's got white trainers
And black trousers, too.
They're my favourite clothes
And my favourite colours, too.*

He's got a blue tracksuit. She's got pink sandals.
a tracksuit, shorts, trainers, sandals, a skirt, a T-shirt, a dress, trousers

p 124   p 108   61

7 Lesson 3 Russ's sandals

1 Think Listen. Where's the story? 🔊 2.61 *See TG notes.*

2 Now watch or listen and read. ▶ 🔊 2.62

1
Come on. Let's walk!
OK.

2
Stop! I'm hot.
Come on, Russ.

3
I'm wearing socks … and boots! My feet are hot!
Take off your boots and socks.

4
I've got an idea.

5
Put on your sandals, Russ.
Wow!
Thank you, Sam!

6
Woof, woof!
Oh no! There's a dog! Hide.

Let's walk! I'm hot. My feet are hot! Take off your boots. Put on your sandals.

62

Lesson 4 **7**

1 Read and tick (✓). Then say.

		Yes	No
1	Stop! I'm cold.	☐	☐
2	I'm wearing trainers.	☐	☐
3	Oh no! There's a cat!	☐	☐
4	It's OK. It's Buddy!	☐	☐

2 Who solves a problem? Look and tick (✓).

3 (Think) Talk about solving problems. *See TG notes.*

p109   63

7 Lesson 5

1 Listen and repeat. Then say. 🔊 2.63

I'm wearing a blue and white T-shirt, purple shorts and green trainers.

I'm wearing an orange T-shirt, a pink skirt and purple sandals.

2 Look, read and write. Then colour.

I'_____ _____ a red T-shirt, green shorts and blue sandals.

I'_____ _____ a pink and white _____ and black _____.

3 Put the words in order. Then number.

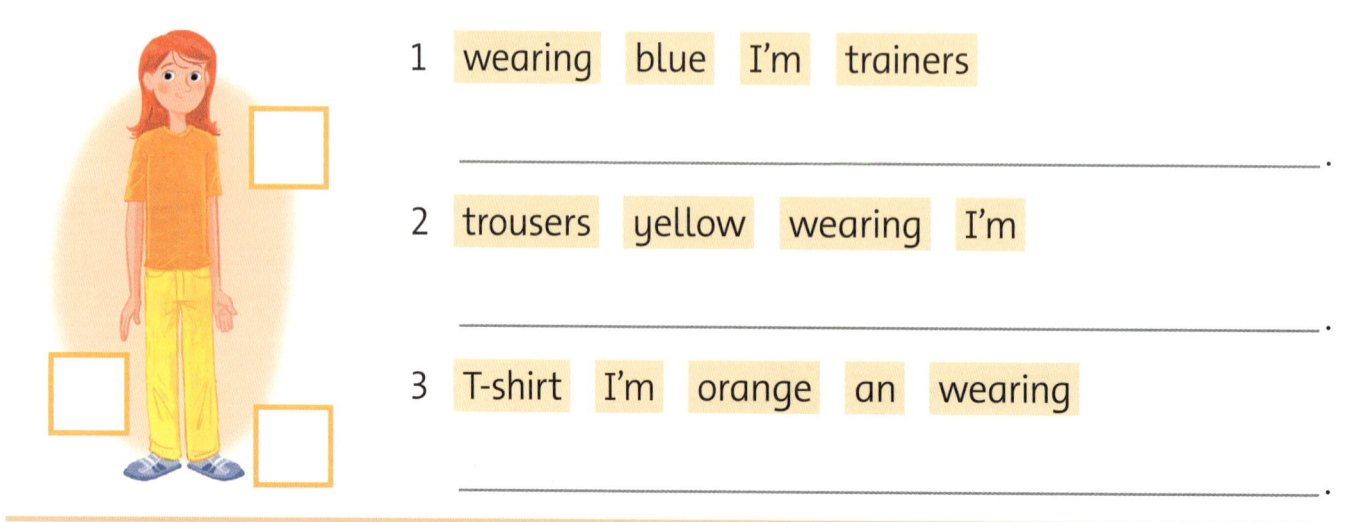

1 wearing   blue   I'm   trainers

_____.

2 trousers   yellow   wearing   I'm

_____.

3 T-shirt   I'm   orange   an   wearing

_____.

I'm wearing a blue and white T-shirt, purple shorts and green trainers.

Grammar p 120   p 110

Lesson 6

7

1 Listen and circle. Then number and colour. 🔊 3.1

2 Read and draw Charlie's clothes. Draw and write for you.

Charlie

I'm Charlie. I'm wearing a yellow T-shirt, red trousers and blue and green trainers.

I'm _____.

Me

3 Play *The Fashion Show Game.* See TG notes.

I'm wearing an orange skirt, a pink T-shirt and white sandals.
a tracksuit, shorts, trainers, sandals, a skirt, a T-shirt, a dress, trousers

p 110

65

Lesson 7 Sound play

1 Listen and repeat. Can you hear the sound? 🔊 3.2

trousers   gloves   trainers

2 Listen and tick (✓) if you hear the sound. 🔊 3.3

flowers ☐   books ☐   ears ☐   eyes ☐   sandals ☐

3 Listen and check. Repeat. 🔊 3.4

4 Listen and say. 🔊 3.5

I'm wearing flowers on my trousers, trainers and gloves.

trousers, gloves, trainers, flowers, ears, eyes, sandals

Lesson 8 Round up 7

1 Listen and number. Then write and say. 🔊 3.6

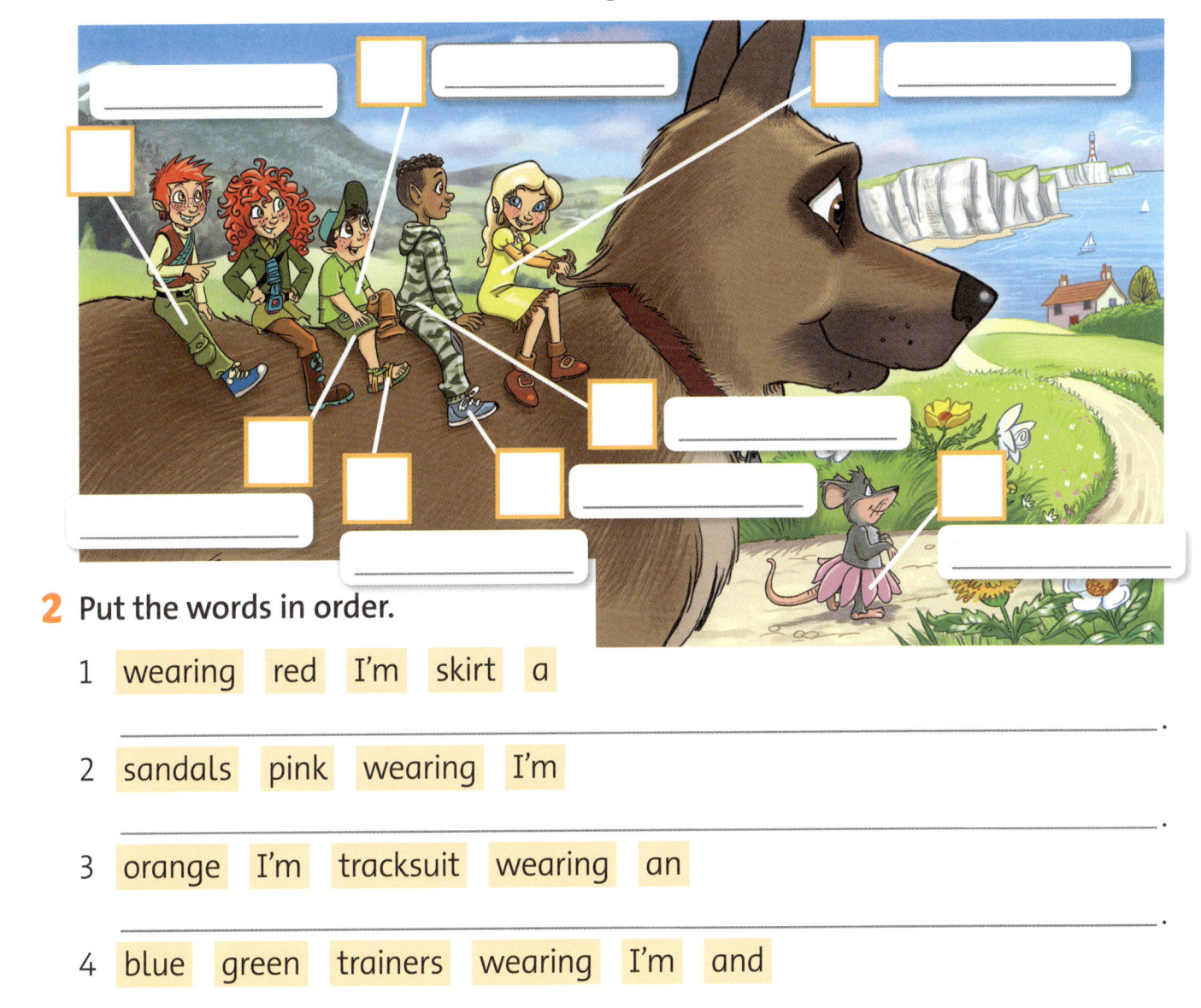

2 Put the words in order.

1. wearing | red | I'm | skirt | a
   _____.
2. sandals | pink | wearing | I'm
   _____.
3. orange | I'm | tracksuit | wearing | an
   _____.
4. blue | green | trainers | wearing | I'm | and
   _____.

3 🏠 **Take Home English** Make a *My clothes* lapbook. *See TG notes.*

This is me. I'm wearing a white T-shirt and grey trousers.

This is me. I'm wearing a yellow and orange dress.

I'm wearing a blue and green tracksuit and black trainers.
a tracksuit, shorts, trainers, sandals, a skirt, a T-shirt, a dress, trousers

8 Sports — Lesson 1

1 Listen and point. Repeat. Write. 🔊 3.7–3.8

2 *Think* Talk about sports. See TG notes.

play football   run   swim   play basketball   dance
ride a bike   do gymnastics   roller skate

3 Chant. 🔊 3.9

4 Play *Sam Says*. See TG notes.

68   play football, run, swim, play basketball, dance, ride a bike, do gymnastics, roller skate   p111

Lesson 2 — 8

1 Look, circle and write.

1. I can / **can't**
  ———————.

2. I can / can't
  ———————.

3. I can / can't
  ———————.

4. I can / can't
  ———————.

5. I can / can't
  ———————.

6. I can / can't
  ———————.

7. I can / can't
  ———————.

8. I can / can't
  ———————.

2 Sing *The Cool Sports Song*. 3.10–3.11

*I love sports. I love sports.
I love to dance and run.
I play football at the beach.
It's great and really fun.
I love sports. I love sports.
I ride my bike all day.
I love sports at the beach.
Can you come and play? Hooray!*

*Let's dance at the beach.
Dance, dance, dance.
Let's play basketball.
Hip, hip, hooray!
Let's roller skate.
It's so great. Oh yeah, oh yeah.*

I can swim. I can't dance.
play football, run, swim, play basketball, dance, ride a bike, do gymnastics, roller skate

p124   p111

69

8 Lesson 3 Hello, Dickin!

1 Think Listen. Where's the story? 🔊 3.12 *See TG notes.*

2 Now watch or listen and read. ▶ 🔊 3.13

1 Look, there are lots of houses. It's Sea Town!

2 Ah, a river! Can you swim, Poppy? Yes, I can.

3 Can you swim, Rowan? No, I can't. No problem. Buddy can swim!

4 Look, who's that? It's Dickin!

5 Hello, Dickin! He's got a message.

6 Come on! Follow Dickin!

A river! No problem! Who's that? He's got a message. Follow Dickin! At last!

Lesson 4

7 Look! It's …

8 Will! And Emily! At last!

1 Look and number. What happens?

a b c
d 1 e f

2 Who's your favourite character? Look and tick (✓).

3 Think Talk about the characters and the stories. *See TG notes.*

p 112

71

8 Lesson 5

1 Listen and repeat. Then ask and answer. 🔊 3.14

Can you play football?
Yes, I can.
No, I can't.

2 Look and write.

1 <u>Can</u> <u>you</u> play football?   Yes, _____ _____.
2 _____ _____ ride a bike?   No, _____ _____.
3 _____ _____ do gymnastics?   _____, _____ _____.
4 _____ _____ dance?   _____, _____ _____.
5 _____ _____ play basketball?   _____, _____ _____.
6 _____ _____ roller skate?   _____, _____ _____.

Can you swim? Yes, I can. No, I can't.

Grammar p 121   p 113

Lesson 6

1 Listen and tick (✓) or cross (✗). 🔊 3.15

2 Ask and answer. Tick (✓) or cross (✗).

	⚽	🏃	🥽	🏀	🚲	🛼	🤸	👟
Friend 1								
Friend 2								
Me								

3 Look and write. Then write and draw about you.

I _____ run, but I _____ _____ _____. My favourite sport is _____.

_____ _____ play basketball?

I _____, but
I _____.
My favourite sport is _____.
Can _____?

Can you play football? Yes, I can. No, I can't.
play football, run, swim, play basketball, dance, ride a bike, do gymnastics, roller skate

p 113

73

8 Lesson 7 Sound play

1 Listen and repeat. Can you hear the sound? 🔊 3.16

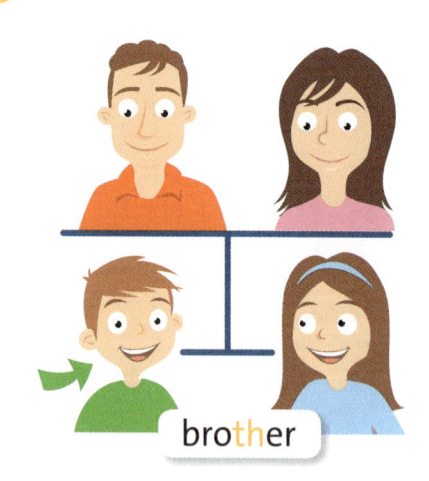

wea**th**er   fa**th**er   bro**th**er

2 Listen and tick (✓) if you hear the sound. 🔊 3.17

mo**th**er ☐   fea**th**er ☐   ba**th**room ☐   clo**th**es ☐   bir**th**day ☐

3 Listen and check. Repeat. 🔊 3.18

4 Listen and say. 🔊 3.19

Can you dance like a feather in this hot weather?

weather, father, brother, mother, feather, clothes

74

Lesson 8 Round up

1 Listen and number. Then write and say. 🔊 3.20

2 Write.

1 _____ 🛼 _____ ? ✓ _____ , _____ .
2 _____ 🏀 _____ ? ✗ _____ , _____ .
3 _____ 🚲 _____ ? ✓ _____ , _____ .
4 _____ 🏃 _____ ? ✓ _____ , _____ .

3 🏠 **Take Home English** Make a *My sports* lapbook. *See TG notes.*

"Can you roller skate?"

"No, I can't."

"Yes, I can. Can you swim?"

4 Play *The Rainbow Bridge Game. See TG notes.*

Can you ride a bike? Yes, I can. No, I can't.
play football, run, swim, play basketball, dance, ride a bike, do gymnastics, roller skate

75

CLIL Science — The water cycle

1 Watch the video. ▶ See TG notes.

2 **Think** Talk about water. See TG notes.

3 Listen and point. Repeat. Write. 🔊 3.21–3.22

1 _____
2 _____
3 _____
4 _____
5 _____
6 _____

sea
rain
vapour
cloud
snow
ice

4 Look, write and circle.

solid   liquid   gas

1 _____Ice_____ is a (solid) / liquid / gas .
2 _____ is a solid / liquid / gas .
3 _____ is a solid / liquid / gas .
4 _____ is a solid / liquid / gas .
5 The _____ is a solid / liquid / gas .

sea   Rain
~~Ice~~   Snow
Vapour

Ice is a solid. Rain is a liquid. Vapour is a gas.
sea, rain, vapour, cloud, snow, ice

76

The water cycle

1 Sing *The Water Cycle Song*. 🔊 3.23–3.24

The water cycle goes round and round.
Vapour goes up and rain comes down.
Rivers take water back to the sea.
Learn the water cycle together with me!

When vapour goes up from the sea to the sun,
That's evaporation, number one.
When clouds form in the sky above you,
That's condensation, number two.
When rain comes down over the trees,
That's precipitation, number three.
When rain fills the rivers more and more,
That's collection, number four.

2 Label the water cycle process.

- evaporation
- condensation
- precipitation
- collection

3 Number and write. Say.

That's evaporation. The water is a gas.

gas

CLIL Science project Make a water cycle diorama. *See TG notes.*

The water is a solid / a liquid / a gas. That's precipitation.
evaporation, condensation, precipitation, collection

CLIL Science

Healthy eating

1 Watch the video. ▶ See TG notes.

2 **Think** Talk about food. See TG notes.

3 Listen and point. Repeat. Match. 🔊 3.25–3.26

1 2 3 4 5

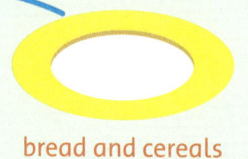

fruit and vegetables   meat and fish   sugary foods   bread and cereals   milk and dairy

4 Look and write.

grapes   spaghetti   milk   carrots   rice   chicken
cheese   apples   cake   chocolate

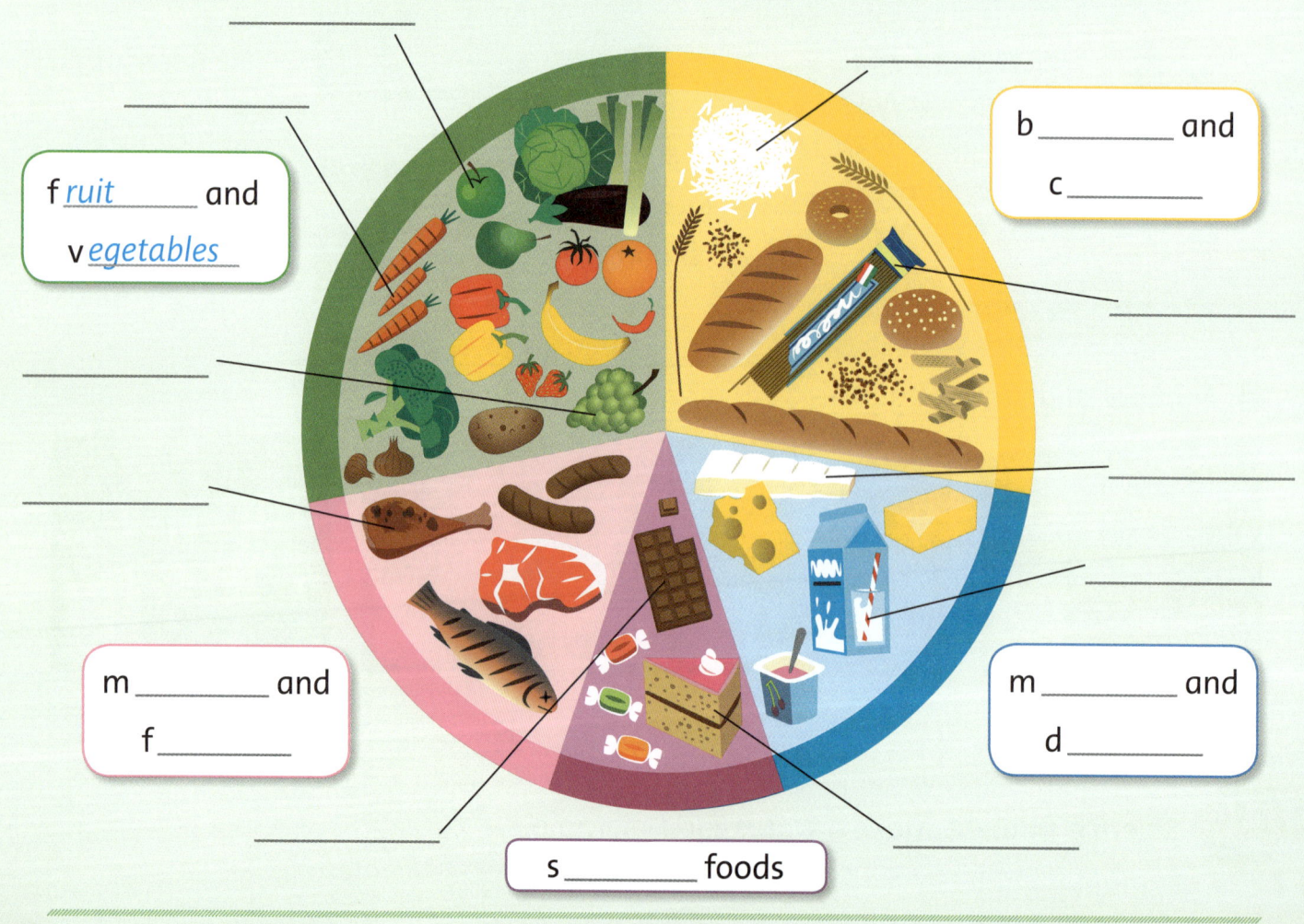

f _ruit_ and v_egetables_

b_____ and c_____

m_____ and f_____

m_____ and d_____

s_____ foods

What's in the yellow group?
fruit and vegetables, meat and fish, sugary foods, bread and cereals, milk and dairy

Healthy eating

1 Sing *The Good for You Song*. 🔊 3.27–3.28

It's the good for you song.
The good for you song.
Come on, sing along!
Let's find out what's good for you.
It's good for you, it's good for me, too!

Fruit and vegetables are good for you.
I like carrots and apples, too.
Salads and orange juice are so yummy.
Fruit and vegetables are good for your tummy.

2 Circle *good* or *not good*. Write and say.

1 crisps    2 fish    3 grapes    4 cola    5 milk    6 sweets

1 ___Crisps___ aren't good for you.
2 _____ is good for you.
3 _____ are good for you.
4 _____ isn't good for you.
5 _____ is good for you.
6 _____ aren't good for you.

3 Draw your meals. Is it good for you? Say.

Milk is good for you.

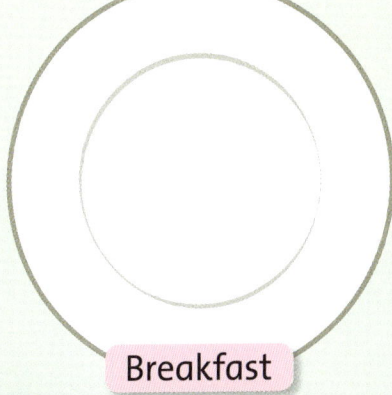

Breakfast    Lunch    Dinner

CLIL Science project Make a five a day chart. *See TG notes.*

Milk is good for you. Cola isn't good for you. Grapes are good for you. Crisps aren't good for you.

p 124

CLIL Citizenship: Recycling

1 Watch the video. ▶ *See TG notes.*

2 **Think** Talk about recycling. *See TG notes.*

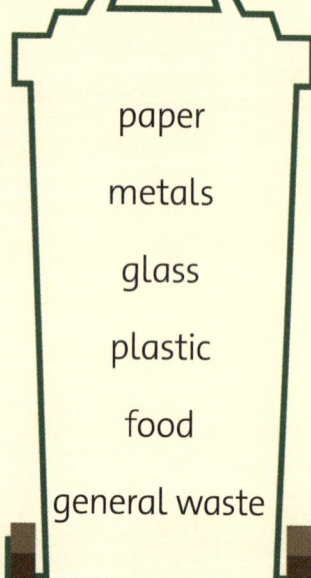

3 Listen and point. Repeat. Write. 🔊 3.29–3.30

paper
metals
glass
plastic
food
general waste

1 _____
2 _____
3 _____
4 _____
5 _____
6 _____

4 Look and number. Then write.

PAPER ___
GLASS 1
GENERAL WASTE ___
FOOD ___
PLASTIC and METALS ___

1 Crisp packets go in the __general__ __waste__ bin.

2 Fruit and vegetables go in the _____ bin.

3 Comics go in the _____ bin.

4 Lemonade cans go in the _____ and _____ bin.

5 Glass bottles go in the _____ bin.

Crisp packets go in the general waste bin.
glass, paper, general waste, food, plastic, metals

80

Recycling

1 Sing *The Rubbish Truck Song.* 🔊 3.31–3.32

Here comes the rubbish truck.
Say hello to the driver, wave good luck!
Let's recycle our rubbish today.
Crash, bang, wallop. Hip, hip, hooray!

Comics go in the paper bin.
Cans go in the metals bin.
Glass bottles go in the glass bin.
Think before you throw it away,
So we can use it another day.

2 Look and write.   rubbish   bottle   recycle   ~~bin~~

1 Plastic bottles go in the plastic ___bin___.
2 The _____ truck takes it away.
3 Let's _____!
4 A plastic _____ becomes a plastic cup.

3 Look and say.   *A comic becomes a book.*

becomes

CLIL Citizenship project *The Recycling Game.* See TG notes.

Comics go in the paper bin. Let's recycle! A comic becomes a book.

CLIL Geography: Landscapes

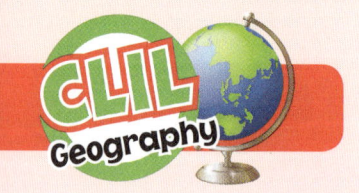

1 Watch the video. ▶ See TG notes.

2 Think Talk about where you live. See TG notes.

3 Listen and point. Repeat. Write. 🔊 3.33–3.34

> a lake   a river   woods   mountains   cliffs   a beach

4 Look and write.

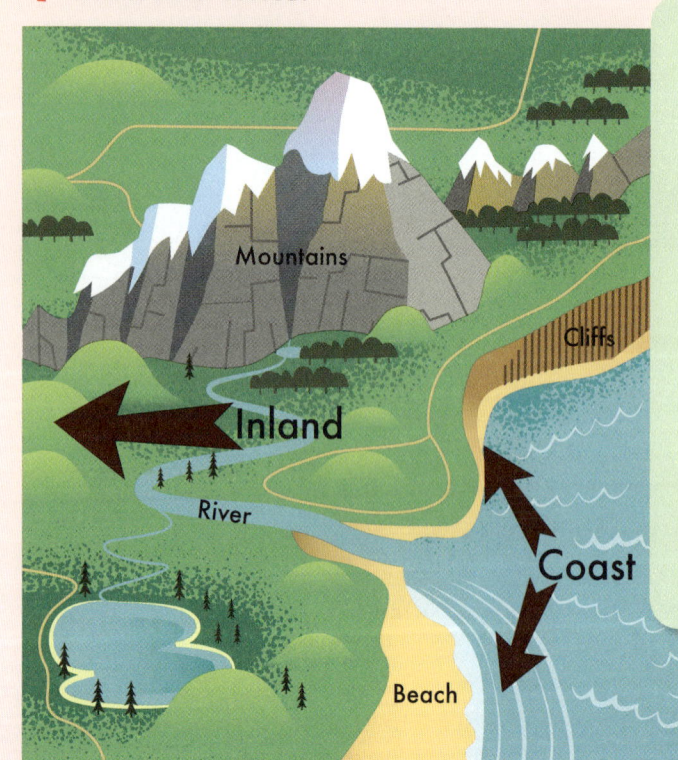

> lakes   ~~cliffs~~   rivers   beaches

1 ____Cliffs____ and _____ are on the coast.

2 _____ and most mountains are inland.

3 _____ start inland and end on the coast.

Cliffs are on the coast. Lakes are inland.
woods, a lake, a river, mountains, cliffs, a beach, inland, coast

Landscapes

CLIL Geography

1 Sing *The Awesome World Song.* 🔊 3.35–3.36

Inland lakes and rivers,
Natural cliffs and beaches.
There are so many things to do and see
In this awesome world, for you and me.

Let's climb a mountain.
Let's walk in the woods.
Let's swim in a man-made lake.
In this awesome world, for you and me.

2 Write.

Man-made	Natural
a house	mountains

~~a house~~
~~mountains~~
a beach   woods
a river   a road
a park   a canal
cliffs
a playground
sea   a bridge

3 Look and say. *Big Ben is man-made. Cliffs are natural.*

Big Ben    cliffs    a town    the Atlantic    a canal

CLIL Geography project My local area. *See TG notes.*

Big Ben is man-made. Cliffs are natural.
woods, a lake, a river, mountains, cliffs, a beach, inland, coast

83

Culture — Food and me!

1 Listen and number the pictures. 🔊 3.37
2 Listen again and write the words. 🔊 3.38

cake and ice cream   ~~roast chicken~~
fish and chips   rice and curry

Hello, I'm Hannah. Let's talk about food!

On Sunday, we eat a roast dinner. It's _roast_ _chicken_, roast potatoes and carrots. My family eats together. This is my dad, my mum, my brother and me!

It's a birthday party! We eat sandwiches and crisps. We eat _____ _____ _____, too. Look at the birthday cake. It's got sweets on top – yum!

This is my favourite restaurant. It's an Indian restaurant. We eat _____ _____ _____. Do you like Indian food?

84

Food and me! Culture

In summer, we go to the beach! We go to the takeaway shop and we eat _____ _____ _____.

We eat on the beach. It's fun!

3 Write *Yes* or *No*.

1. There's rice at the restaurant. — Yes
2. Hannah eats fish and pizza in summer. — ____
3. Roast dinner is roast chicken and potatoes. — ____
4. There are apples on the birthday cake. — ____

4 (Think) Look at the photos. Is it the same or different where you live? *See TG notes.*

Culture

Project Make a birthday party plate. *See TG notes.*

"This is my favourite party food. We eat sandwiches, grapes and cupcakes!"

"This is my favourite party food. We eat sweets, ice cream and cake!"

This is my favourite party food. We eat sandwiches and crisps.
roast chicken, roast potatoes, a birthday cake, sweets, a restaurant, curry, chips

Culture — Sport and dance and me!

1 Listen and number the pictures. 🔊 3.39
2 Listen again and write the words. 🔊 3.40

play cricket   do karate
do street dance   do ballet

Hello, I'm Harry. Let's talk about sport and dance!

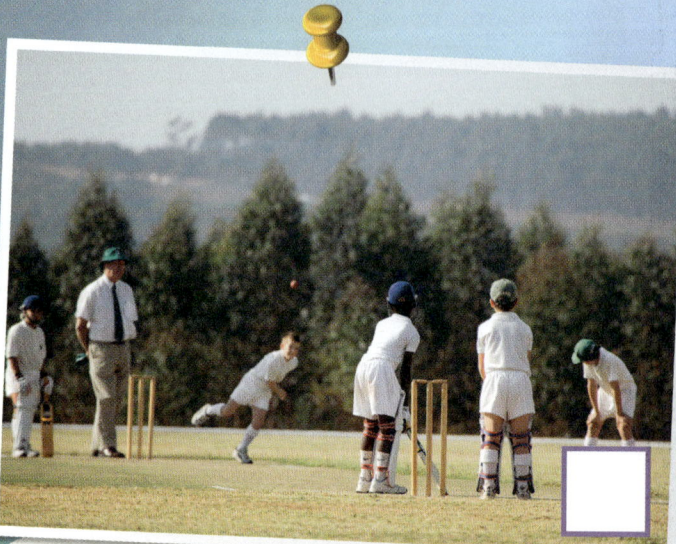

After school, I _____ _____. Karate class is indoors. Look at the uniform. It's white. Karate is fun. I can jump and fly – watch out!

In summer, I _____ _____. We play outdoors, on the grass. I'm wearing white shorts and a white T-shirt. I've got a cricket bat and a ball.

This is my sister's ballet class. She can dance very well. Lots of girls _____ _____, but boys can do ballet, too. The girls are wearing pink and black clothes and pink shoes.

86

Sport and dance and me! Culture

I can't do ballet, but I can dance. I ___ ___ ___.

This is a performance indoors. In street dance, we can jump, hop and do gymnastics. I love it!

3 Write *Yes* or *No*.

1 I'm wearing black trousers for cricket.   *No*
2 Ballet clothes are pink and black.   ___
3 I do karate outdoors.   ___
4 Boys can do ballet.   ___

4 (Think) Look at the photos. Is it the same or different where you live? *See TG notes.*

Project Draw a picture of you doing your favourite after-school activity. *See TG notes.*

After school, I play football. I'm wearing a blue T-shirt and pink shorts.

After school, I do street dance. I'm wearing a red tracksuit and trainers.

After school, I do karate. I'm wearing white shorts. I've got a bat and ball. I can't do ballet, but I can dance.
play cricket, do karate, do street dance, do ballet, uniform, indoors, outdoors, performance

87

It's Christmas Eve!

1 Listen and point. Repeat. 🔊 3.41–3.42

1	2	3	4
a stocking	a fireplace	mince pies	a letter

2 Read the words. Listen and write. Then listen and check. 🔊 3.43

> reindeer   presents   stocking   mince pies
> fireplace   tree   letter   Father Christmas

1 There are lights and baubles on the Christmas _____.

2 There are _____ under the tree.

3 On Christmas Eve, I hang my _____.

4 We hang stockings on the _____.

5 I put out _____ _____ and a carrot for Father Christmas and the _____.

6 I write a _____ to _____ _____.

3 Listen and draw. Then colour. 🔊 3.44

4 Play *The Christmas Stockings Game.* See TG notes.

5 Make and decorate a Christmas stocking. See TG notes.

There are presents under the tree. I hang my stocking.
Christmas Eve, a stocking, a fireplace, mince pies, a letter, a reindeer, baubles, Father Christmas

It's Easter time!

1 Look, listen and match. 🔊 3.45

1. Max
2. Daria
3. Adam
4. Sophia

Ukraine Germany Greece Hungary

2 Read and decorate the Easter eggs.

1 There's yellow dye on this egg. There's a brown Easter bunny with pink ears and a pink nose.

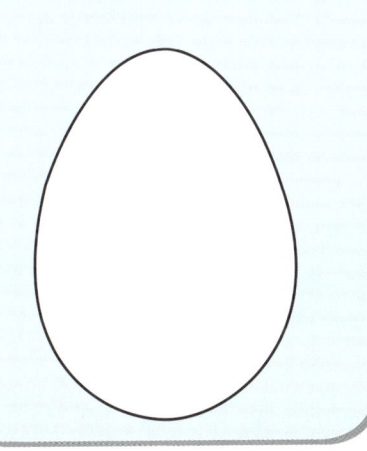

2 There's a pattern on this egg. There's a blue triangle, a pink circle, a blue triangle and a pink circle.

3 There's purple, red and green paint on this egg. There are two purple flowers and two red flowers. There are four green leaves.

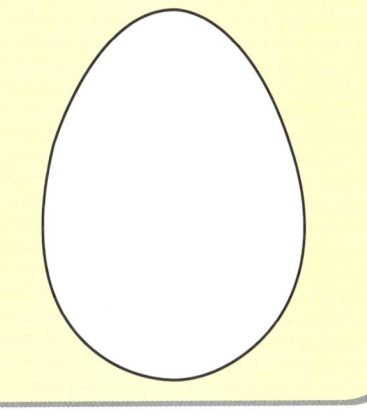

4 Play *The Easter Egg Game.* See TG notes. **5** Decorate or paint an Easter egg. See TG notes.

There's yellow dye on this egg. There are two purple flowers.
Easter eggs, decorate, paint, dye, pattern, a circle, a triangle

1 Lessons 1 and 2

1 Read and match.

1 a bookshop
2 a clothes shop
3 a school
4 a playground
5 a post office
6 a police station

a
b
c
d
e
f

2 Look and write.

bookshop   police station   playground   school
post office   clothes shop   cafe   ~~toy shop~~

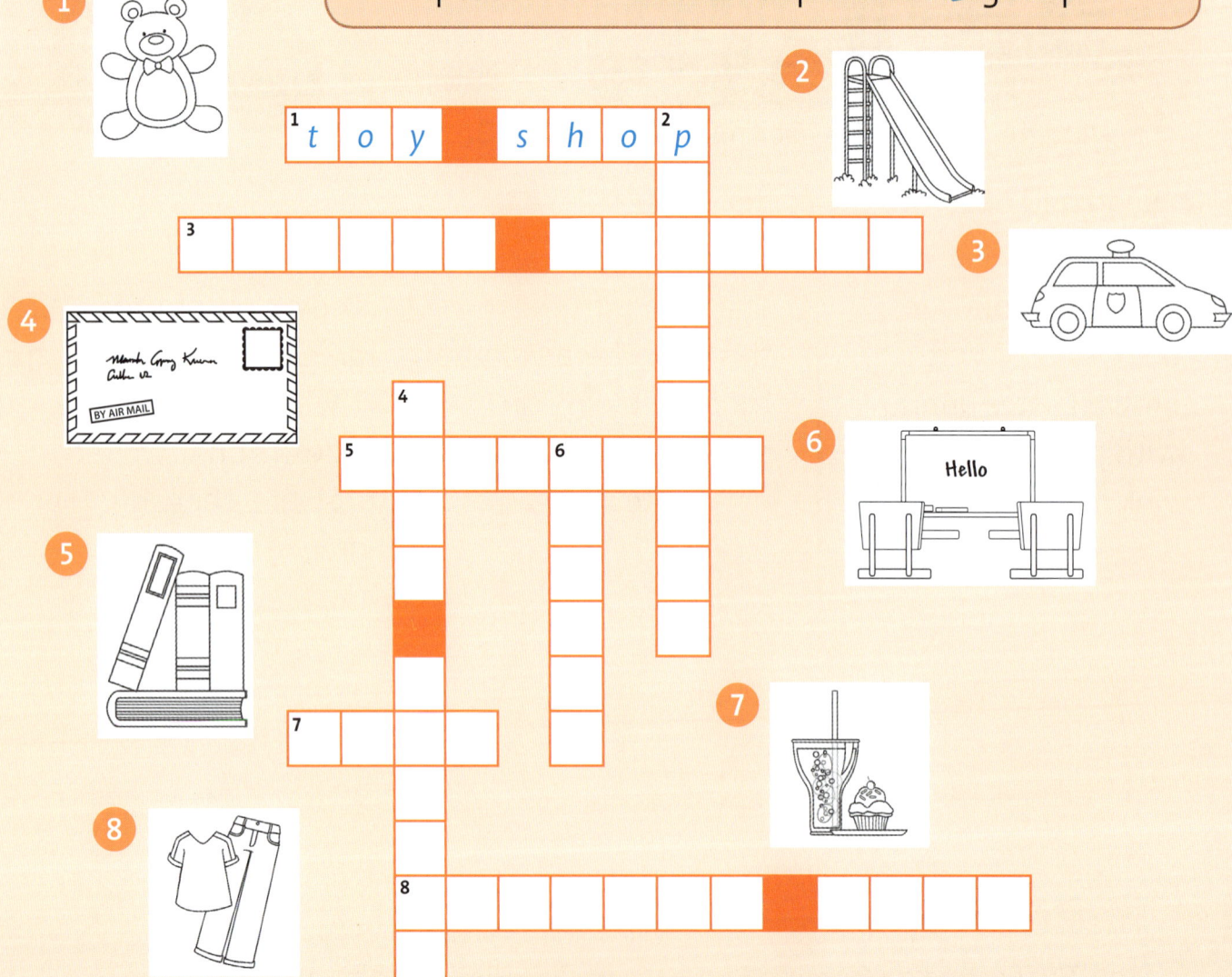

1. t o y   s h o p
2.
3.
4.
5.
6.
7.
8.

90   a bookshop, a police station, a cafe, a playground, a toy shop, a school, a post office, a clothes shop

Lesson 4

1 Read and circle.

1. I've got my car / **bike**. 
2. Look, there's a **police station** / post office. 
3. Uh oh. It's my **brother** / sister! 
4. Aargh! **Climb** / Jump!

2 Can you remember? What colour is Will's bike? Colour.

3 Look and tick (✓) Poppy being calm.

I'm bored. Let's go to town. Hide! Jump! Is it the cafe? No, it isn't! Come back!

91

1 Lessons 5 and 6

1 Put the words in order. Then number.

1. a school There's _____.
2. toy shop There's a _____.
3. There are trees lots of _____.
4. a There's police station _____.
5. three cars There are _____.
6. post offices two There are _____.

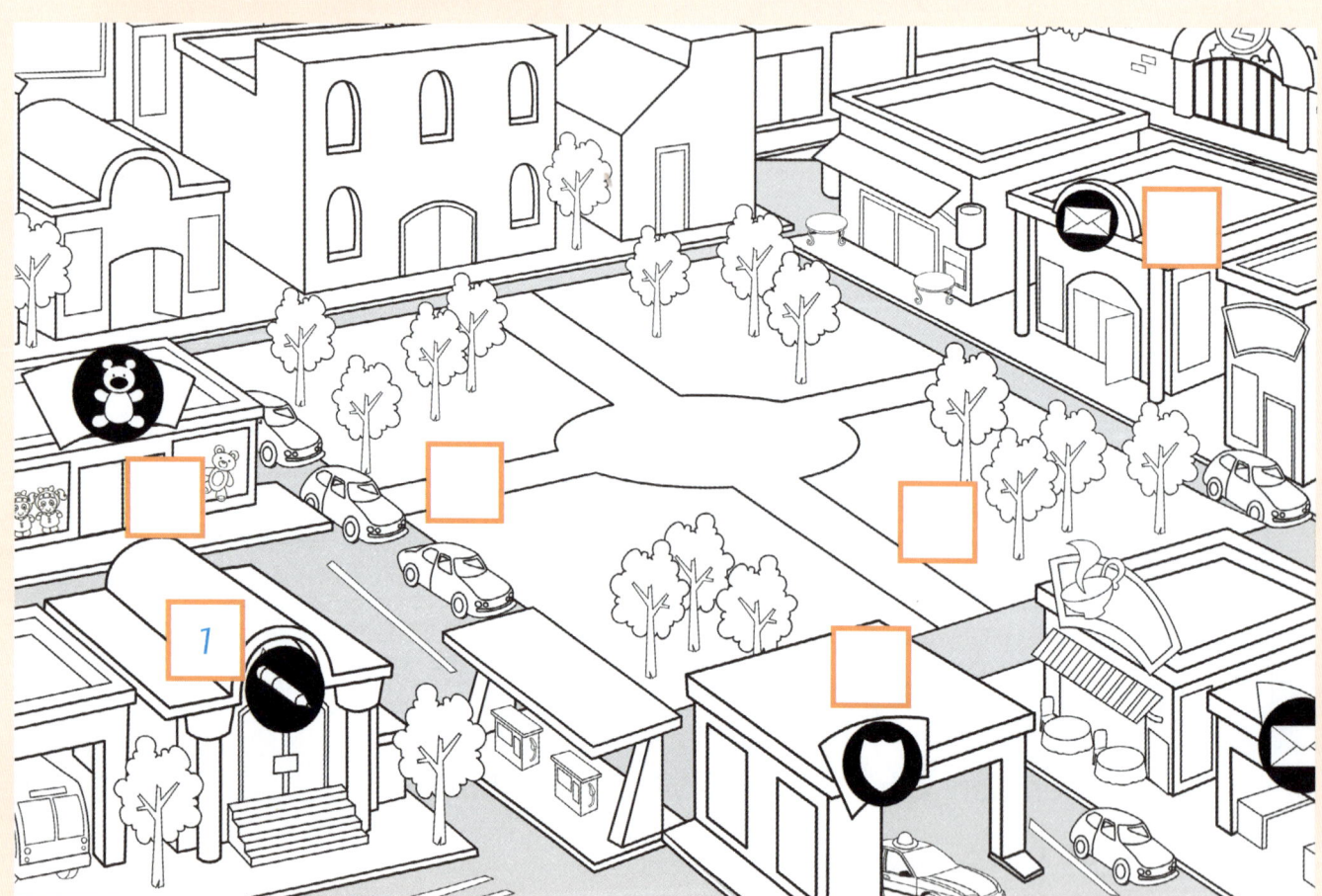

2 Write *There's* or *There are*. Then look and circle.

1. ___There are___ four **bookshops** / **clothes shops**.
2. _____ lots of **cafes** / **toy shops**.
3. _____ a **playground** / **police station**.
4. _____ three **post offices** / **schools**.

There's a school. There are three cars. There are lots of trees.

92

Lessons 1 and 2

1 Match. Then write the words in order.

eleven
_____
_____
_____
_____
_____
_____
_____
_____
twenty

2 Complete. Then write the numbers.

| 11 | 14 | 15 | 16 | ~~19~~ | 20 |

1. 10 + 9 = *19* *nineteen*
2. 17 − 3 = ____ _____
3. 7 + 4 = ____ _____
4. 20 − 5 = ____ _____
5. 18 + 2 = ____ _____
6. 17 − 1 = ____ _____

eleven, twelve, thirteen, fourteen, fifteen, sixteen, seventeen, eighteen, nineteen, twenty

2 Lesson 4

1 Read, choose and write.

> eight   catch   eighteen   ~~name~~

1. What's your ___name___?
2. I'm _____.
3. It's number _____.
4. Sniff, _____!

2 Can you remember? What number boat are Fern, Poppy and Rowan on?

Write. _____

3 Look and tick (✓) making a new friend.

Hello!
What's your name?

It's the boat. No, it isn't. It's number 18! Come on, Sniff! Catch!

94

Lessons 5 and 6 2

1 Write questions and answers. Then match.

How   Where   What

1 _____ are you from?
2 _____'s your name?
3 _____ old are you?

a _____ eight.
b _____ Bridge Town.
c _____ Rowan.

2 Write about Will. Then write about you and draw.

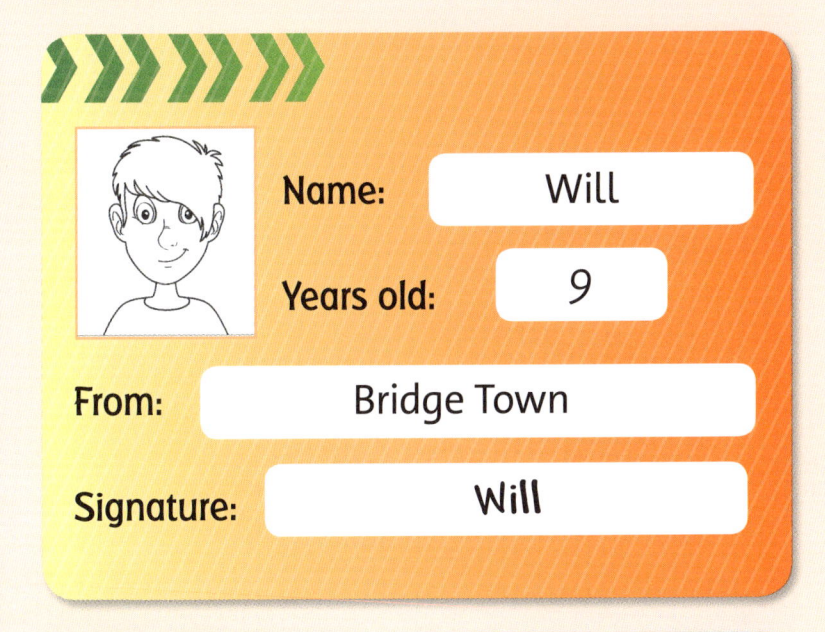

Name: Will
Years old: 9
From: Bridge Town
Signature: Will

My _____ Will.
I'm _____
_____.
I'm from _____
_____.

Name: _____
Years old: _____
From: _____
Signature: _____

My _____
_____
_____
_____
_____.

What's your name? My name's … How old are you? I'm … Where are you from? I'm from …

95

3 Lessons 1 and 2

1 Find and circle. Then match.

chickenjavsaladhsgbreadnispaghettiqsdricej
kofishpidymilkaofsoupbxm

2 Look and write. Which foods are missing? Say.

1. _____
2. _____
3. _____
4. _____
5. _____
6. _____

Missing:
_____
_____

spaghetti, salad, rice, fish, milk, bread, chicken, soup

96

Lesson 4

1 Look, read and number. Then say.

1. Do you like salad?
   - ☐ Orange juice, Rowan?
   - [1] Yes, I like salad.

2. Will!
   - ☐ Hello, everyone!
   - ☐ I've got sandwiches and juice.

3. This is Emily.

4. Yuck!

2 Can you remember? What food doesn't Fern like? Write. _____

3 Write the missing words. Is Russ being polite?

you   Fish   thank

_____, Russ?

No, _____ _____.

Where's Will? I'm hungry. I'm thirsty. This is Emily. Sorry. No, thank you.

97

3 Lessons 5 and 6

1 Look and write.

I like _____ and _____.
I don't like _____.

I like _____ and _____.
I don't like _____.

2 Look. Write questions and answers.

1 Do you like _____, Will?
   Yes, I like _____.

2 _____, Emily?
   _____.

3 _____, Sniff?
   _____.

4 _____, Poppy?
   _____.

Do you like rice? Yes, I like rice. No, I don't like rice.

98

Lessons 1 and 2

1 Find, circle and write.

k	e	y	r	i	n	g	s	r	p
w	r	t	y	c	u	i	o	p	u
z	x	c	v	e	g	h	y	u	z
v	c	h	j	c	y	e	w	r	z
e	o	r	t	r	y	b	a	l	l
t	m	u	I	e	u	i	k	q	e
x	i	f	c	a	r	h	u	i	l
d	c	h	j	m	i	v	x	z	d
k	l	d	o	l	l	r	q	t	s
a	p	o	s	t	c	a	r	d	b

1. *ice cream*
2. ___
3. ___
4. ___
5. ___ 
6. ___ 
7. ___ 
8. ___

2 Look and write.

1. *ten*
2. ___ 
3. ___ 
4. ___ 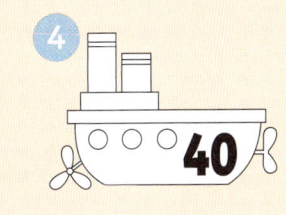
5. ___ 
6. ___ 
7. ___ 
8. ___ 
9. ___ 
10. ___

a key ring, an ice cream, a car, a doll, a comic, a ball, a postcard, a puzzle
ten, twenty, thirty, forty, fifty, sixty, seventy, eighty, ninety, one hundred

99

Lesson 4

1 Read, choose and write. Then order the story.

Help   Poppy   idea   doll

a) ___Help___ me!

b) I've got an _____. Wait here!   **1**

c) Mum, look! It's a _____.

d) _____, come back!

2 Can you remember? How much is an ice cream in the story?

Write. _____

3 Poppy doesn't follow instructions. Tick (✓) what happens.

It's cold! I've got an idea. Wait here! Help me! It's a doll. Here's the ice cream!

Lessons 5 and 6

1 Look and write. Then tick (✓) or cross (✗).

postcard   doll   car   ~~ball~~

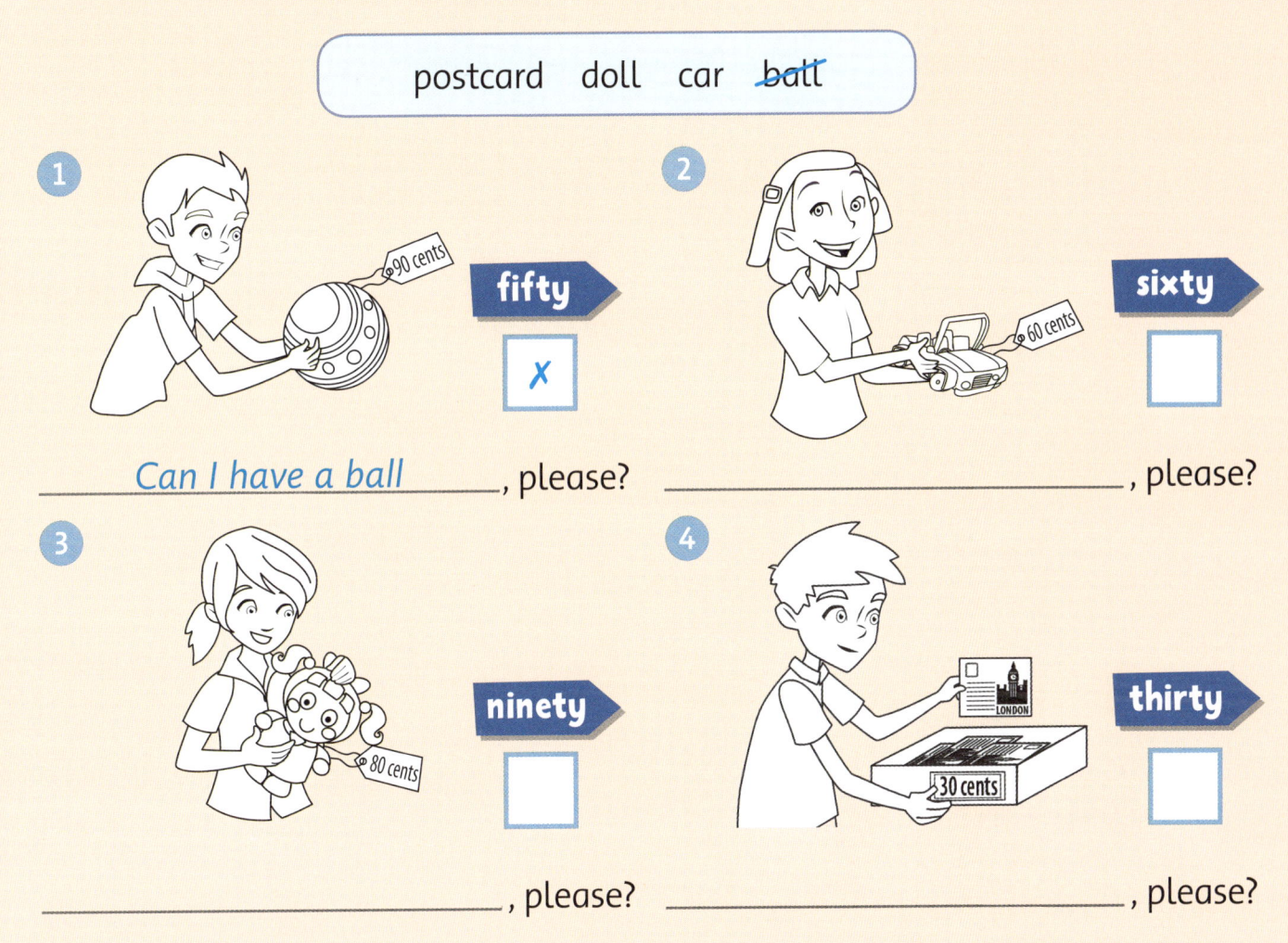

1 fifty ✗

Can I have a ball, please?

2 sixty ☐

_____, please?

3 ninety ☐

_____, please?

4 thirty ☐

_____, please?

2 Look and write.

1 How much is _____ it _____? It's _____ forty _____ cents.
2 How much _____? _____ cents.
3 How _____? _____ cents.
4 _____? _____ cents.

Can I have a key ring, please? Yes, here you are. How much is it? It's forty cents.

101

5 Lessons 1 and 2

1 Write and number.

wardrobe chair bookshelf bed desk lamp rug ~~drawers~~

dr _a_ w _e_ r s [8]

a b ___ d [ ]

a l ___ m ___ [ ]

a b ___ ___ ks ___ elf [ ]

a r ___ g [ ]

a w ___ rdr ___ b ___ [ ]

a c ___ a ___ r [ ]

a d ___ s ___ [ ]

2 Write *There's* or *There are*. Colour.

1 _There's_ an orange rug and _____ two yellow chairs.
2 _____ a brown bookshelf and _____ a pink lamp.
3 _____ a purple desk and _____ green drawers.
4 _____ two blue beds and _____ a white wardrobe.

There's an orange rug, and there are two yellow chairs.
a desk, a bed, a bookshelf, a lamp, a rug, a wardrobe, a chair, drawers

102

Lesson 4

1 Read and circle. Choose and write.

lost   ~~Town~~   There's a   There's a

1 Oh **yes** / **no**! Bridge ___Town___ is the other way!

2 _____ **red** / **green** traffic light.

3 **Please** / **Thank you** help us. We're _____.

4 _____ **phone** / **lamp** on the desk.

2 Can you remember? What does Will's message say? Write and check.

_____

3 Look and tick (✓) helping others.

Bridge Town is the other way! I'm your friend. Please help us. We're lost. Let's send a message!

103

5 Lessons 5 and 6

1 Write *There's* or *There are*. Then look and complete.

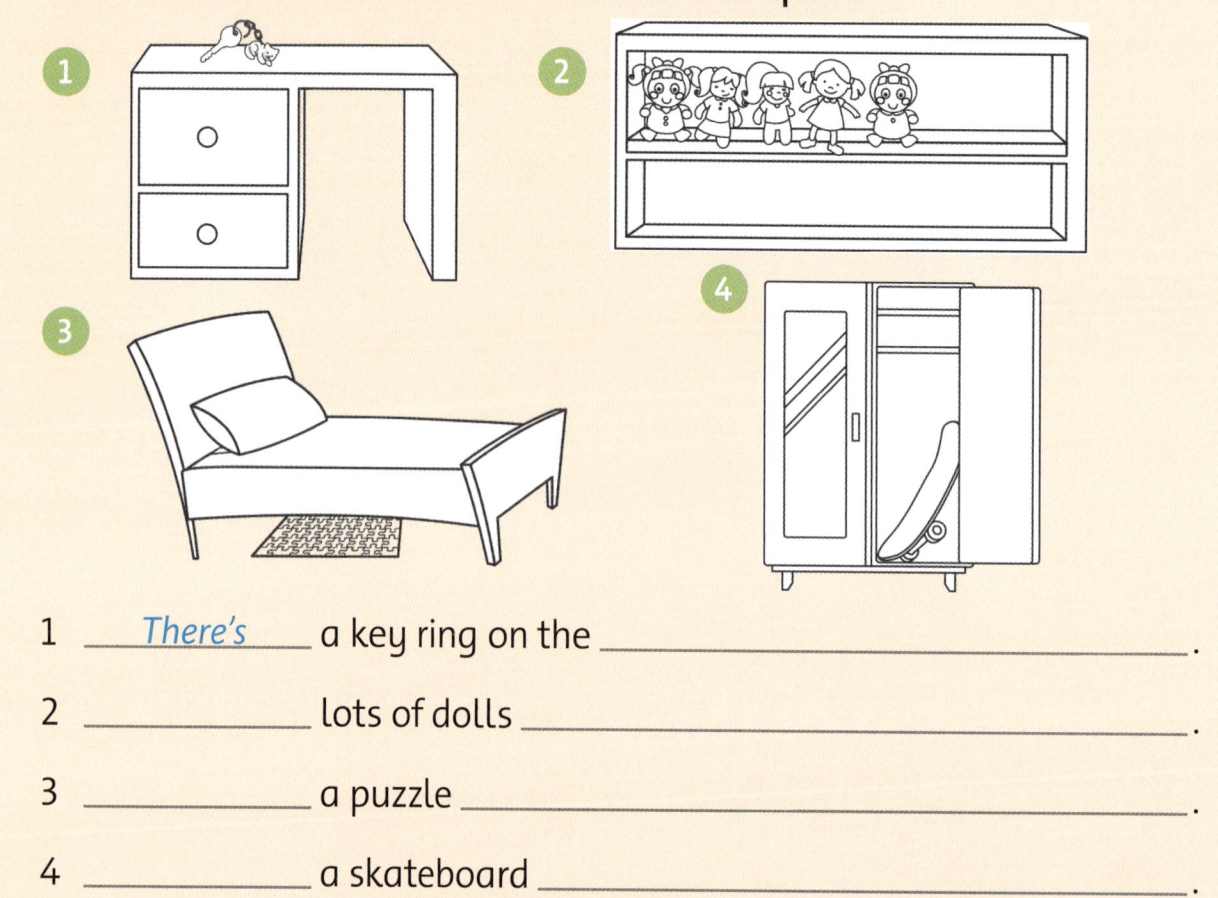

1 __There's__ a key ring on the _____.

2 _____ lots of dolls _____.

3 _____ a puzzle _____.

4 _____ a skateboard _____.

2 Read. What's missing? Draw and colour.

This is my bedroom. There's a yellow bed. There's a brown desk and there are two black chairs. There's a red ball under the desk. There's a purple rug. There's an orange wardrobe and there's a blue bookshelf. There's a green T-shirt in the wardrobe. There are two yellow cars on the bookshelf. I love my bedroom!

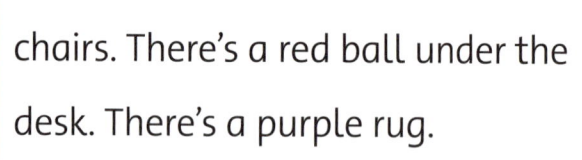

There's a red ball in / on / under the desk. There are cars in / on / under the chair.

104

Lessons 1 and 2 **6**

1 How many? Count and write.

> Frisbees ~~kites~~ rackets tablets poster bikes
> skateboards helmets

1. two kites
2. _____
3. _____
4. _____
5. _____
6. _____
7. _____
8. _____

2 Draw. Then write.

> a skateboard a helmet ~~a racket~~ a tablet a kite a Frisbee a poster a bike

1 I've got _____a racket_____ and _____.
2 I've got _____ and _____.
3 I've got _____ and _____.
4 I've got _____ and _____.

I've got a poster and a tablet.
a racket, a bike, a poster, a helmet, a tablet, a Frisbee, a skateboard, a kite

6 Lesson 4

1 Read, choose and write. Then order the story.

Buddy   Run   kite   ~~skateboard~~

a — Look, he's got a _____.

b — Don't wake _____!

c — Quick! _____!

d — Let's take the _skateboard_. — 1

2 Can you remember? In the story, what's on the poster? Write and draw.

3 Which pictures in activity 1 show teamwork?

Let's take the skateboard. Don't wake Buddy! Ready, steady, go! Humans!

106

Lessons 5 and 6 — 6

1 Read. Look and match.

- He's got a bike and a skateboard.
- She's got a Frisbee and a kite. 
- She's got a racket and a Frisbee. 
- He's got a poster and a skateboard. 

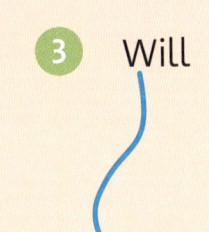

1 Rowan 2 Emily 3 Will 4 Poppy

a 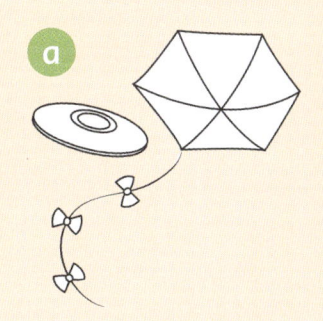 b  c  d

2 Draw and write.

He _____
_____
_____
_____
_____ .

She _____
_____
_____
_____
_____
_____ .

He's got a bike and a skateboard. She's got a racket and a Frisbee.

107

7 Lessons 1 and 2

1 Draw and write.

> a skirt   trousers   a T-shirt   sandals   a tracksuit
> shorts   a dress   trainers

1. 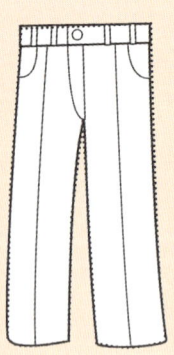
2. 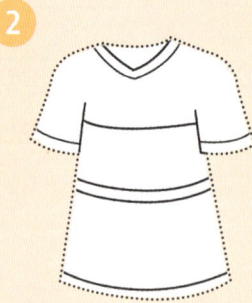
3. 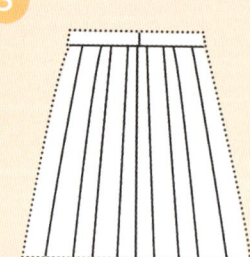
4.

5. 
6. 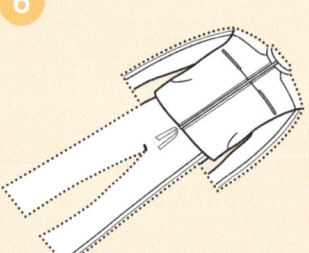
7. 
8.

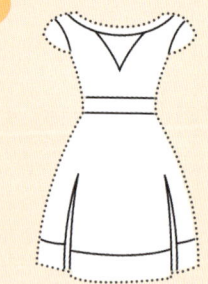

2 Look, circle and write. Then colour.

1 She's got black **sandals** / **trainers**.

   She's got black trainers.

2 She's got a purple **skirt** / **tracksuit**.

3 He's got an orange **dress** / **T-shirt**.

4 He's got yellow **shorts** / **trousers**.

Lesson 4   7

1 Read, choose and write. Then order the story.

> walk   ~~dog~~   sandals   socks

a) Oh no! There's a ___dog___!

b) Put on your _____, Russ!

c) Come on. Let's _____!

d) Take off your boots and _____.

2 Can you remember?
Who is the dog in the story? Write.

_____

3 Can you solve the problem?
It's hot! Draw clothes for Poppy or Rowan.

Let's walk. I'm hot. My feet are hot! Take off your boots. Put on your sandals.

109

7 Lessons 5 and 6

1 Read and number. Then colour.

I'm wearing a purple dress and brown sandals. **3**

I'm wearing blue trousers, a white T-shirt and green boots.

I'm wearing a red T-shirt, a black skirt and yellow shoes.

I'm wearing a green tracksuit and blue trainers.

1　2　3　4

2 Colour. Follow and write.

1 *I'm wearing a black T-shirt and* _____.

2 _____.

3 _____.

4 _____.

I'm wearing a green T-shirt and orange trainers.

Lessons 1 and 2

8

1 Look and write.

ride a bike   do gymnastics   play basketball
swim   play football   roller skate   dance   run

1. _____ 
2. _____ 
3. _____ 
4. _____ 
5. _____ 
6. _____ 
7. _____ 
8. _____

2 Look and write.

	 🚲	 🛼	 👟
Poppy	✓	✗	✓
Sniff	✗	✗	✓

1.  I can _____.
   _____.
   _____.

2. I can't _____.
   _____.
   _____.

I can run. I can't swim.
play football, run, swim, play basketball, dance, ride a bike, do gymnastics, roller skate

111

8 Lesson 4

1 Read, choose and write. Then order the story.

> can't   Emily   houses   message

a Hello, Dickin! He's got a _____.

b Can you swim, Rowan? No, I _____.

c Will! And _____! At last!

d There are lots of _____. It's Sea Town!

2 Can you remember? Who can swim in the story? Write. _____

3 Tick (✓) for you. Can you … ?

1. be calm ☐
2. make friends ☐
3. be polite ☐
4. follow instructions ☐
5. help others ☐
6. work in a team ☐
7. solve problems ☐

A river! No problem! Who's that? He's got a message. Follow Dickin! At last!

112

Lessons 5 and 6   8

1 Look and write.

1 ___Can you swim___, Poppy?   Yes, _____.
2 _____, Russ?   _____.
3 _____, Sam?   _____.
4 _____, Sniff?   _____.

2 Look and write. Answer for you.

1 ___Can you_____? _____.
2 _____? _____.
3 _____? _____.
4 _____? _____.

3 Write about you. Draw.

_____
_____
_____
_____
_____
_____

Can you swim? Yes, I can. No, I can't.

113

1 Extra grammar practice

There's a ruler.

There are three pens.

There's / There are ...

1 Write the words in the correct box.

> four schools   a playground   six cafes
> two toy shops   a post office   a clothes shop

There's _____

_____

_____.

There are _____

_____

_____.

2 Count and write.

1 two | There | cars | are   _____.
2 a | There's | police | station   _____.
3 _____.
4 _____.

Reflection on language: There's / There are ...

Extra grammar practice 2

What's your name?

Where are you from?

How old are you?

Question words

1 Put the words in order. Then match the questions and answers.

1 your | name | What's
_____?

2 old | How | you | are
_____?

3 from | Where | you | are
_____?

a ten | I'm
_____.

b I'm | Bologna | from
_____.

c name's | My | Marco
_____.

2 Write questions with *What*, *Where* and *How*. Write the answers.

_____ your _____?

_____ Lucia.

_____ from?

_____ Florence.

_____?

_____ nine.

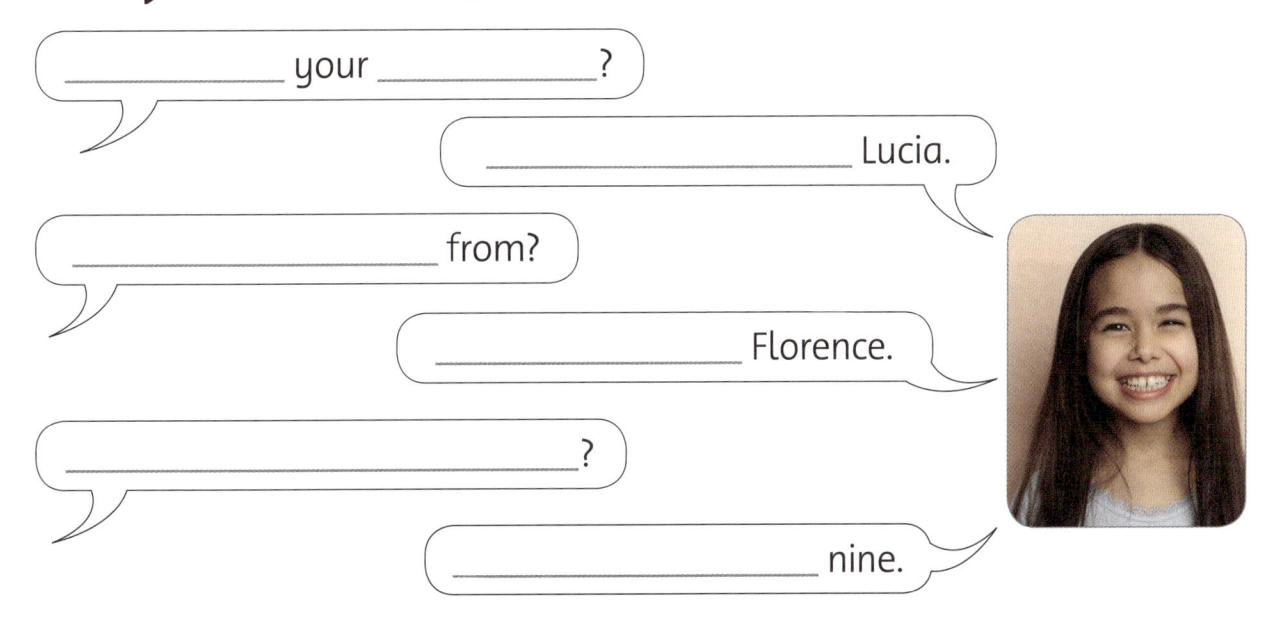

Reflection on language: Question words

115

3 Extra grammar practice

Present simple: like / don't like

1 Put the words in order.

1 you Do soup like _____?
2 like Do fish you _____?
3 like milk Do you _____?
4 like Do salad you _____?
5 you chicken like Do _____?

2 Write answers that are true for you.

1 Do you like [salad] ? _____.
2 Do you like [kiwi] ? _____.
3 Do you like [milk] ? _____.
4 Do you like [soup] ? _____.
5 Do you like [chicken] ? _____.

Reflection on language: Present simple: like / don't like

116

Extra grammar practice 4

Requests, Quantities

1 Put the words in order.

1 I have Can doll, a please _____?
2 puzzle, a please I Can have _____?
3 please have Can comic, I a _____?
4 key ring, a Can I please have _____?

2 Follow to find the prices. Write.

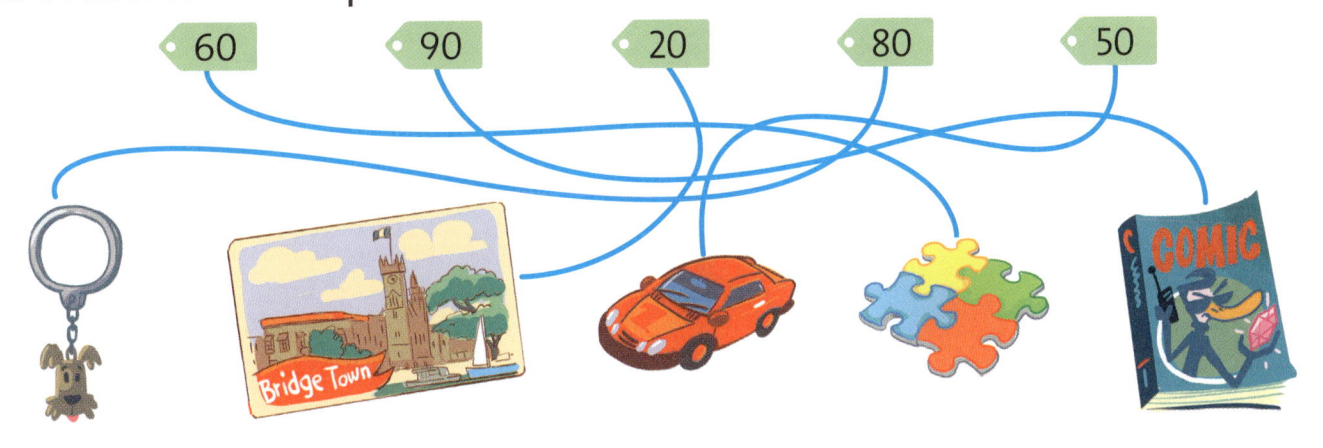

60   90   20   80   50

1 How much is the postcard? _It's_ _____ cents.
2 How much is the car? _____ cents.
3 _____ comic? _____ cents.
4 _____ puzzle? _____ cents.
5 _____ key ring? _____ cents.

Reflection on language: Requests, Quantities

117

5 Extra grammar practice

There's a dog on the bridge.

There's a fish under the bridge.

Prepositions

1 Look and write.

bottle ball train lamp helmet cat   wardrobe bed desk

1 There's _____ *a bottle on the wardrobe* _____ .
2 There's *a ball* _____ .
3 _____ .
4 _____ .
5 _____ .
6 _____ .

2 Say. Ask and answer.   Where's the bottle?   It's on the wardrobe.

Reflection on language: Prepositions

Extra grammar practice 6

Have got

Look at the fish!

He's got a kite!

1 Put the words in order. Then answer for you.

1 you got Have a bike _____? _____.
2 a helmet got Have you _____? _____.
3 you Have Frisbee a got _____? _____.
4 got Have a you tablet _____? _____.

2 Look and write.

1 He's _____. 4 She's _____.
2 _____. 5 _____.
3 _____. 6 _____.

Reflection on language: Have got

7 Extra grammar practice

Present continuous

1 Put the words in order.

1 wearing I'm pink T-shirt a _____.
2 red wearing shorts I'm _____.
3 white and trainers I'm black wearing _____
_____.
4 and a tracksuit blue wearing green I'm _____
_____.

2 Colour and write.

1 *I'm wearing* _____
_____
_____
_____
_____.

2 _____
_____
_____
_____
_____.

Reflection on language: Present continuous

Extra grammar practice 8

Abilities: can / can't

1 Put the words in order.

1 play Can football you _____?
2 do gymnastics you Can _____?
3 run Can you _____?
4 bike a Can ride you _____?

2 Complete. Then answer for you.

1 Can you _____? _____.
2 Can you _____? _____.
3 Can you _____? _____.
4 Can you _____? _____.

Reflection on language: Abilities: can / can't

121

Wordlist

Along the canal
a zebra crossing
a road
a traffic light
a seat belt
a helmet
the pavement
Look left.
Look right.
Stop.
Look.
Listen.
Wait!

Unit 1
a bookshop
a police station
a cafe
a playground
a toy shop
a school
a post office
a clothes shop
I'm bored.
Let's go to town.
Hide!
Jump!
Is it the cafe?
No, it isn't.
Come back!
There's a school.
There are three bikes.
There are lots of leaves.

Unit 2
eleven
twelve
thirteen
fourteen
fifteen
sixteen
seventeen
eighteen
nineteen
twenty
It's the boat.
No, it isn't.
It's number 18!
Come on, Sniff!
Catch!
What's your name?
My name's ...
How old are you?
I'm ...
Where are you from?
I'm from ...

At the station
passengers
icicles
a help point
a train driver
a train
a police officer
Keep safe.
Hold hands.
Ask for help.

Unit 3
spaghetti
salad
rice
fish
milk
bread
chicken
soup
Where's Will?
I'm hungry.
I'm thirsty.
This is Emily.
Sorry.
No, thank you.
Do you like spaghetti?
Yes, I like spaghetti.
No, I don't like spaghetti.

Unit 4
a key ring
an ice cream
a car
a doll
a comic
a ball
a postcard
a puzzle
ten
twenty
thirty
forty
fifty
sixty
seventy
eighty
ninety
one hundred
It's cold!
I've got an idea.
Wait here!
It's a doll.
Help me!
Here's the ice cream!
Can I have a postcard, please?
Yes, here you are.
How much is it?
It's 20 cents.

In the woods
litter
a bin
a plastic bag
a sign
a bottle
a can
Don't drop litter.
Pick up your bottle.
Put it in the bin.

Unit 5
a desk
a bed
a bookshelf
a lamp
a rug
a wardrobe
a chair
drawers
There's a blue bed and there are two yellow bookshelves.
Bridge Town is the other way.
I'm your friend.
Please help us.
We're lost.
Let's send a message.
There's a phone in / on / under the desk.
There are books in / on / under the wardrobe.

Unit 6
a racket
a bike
a poster
a helmet
a tablet
a Frisbee
a skateboard
a kite
I've got a poster and a tablet.
Let's take the skateboard.
Don't wake Buddy.
Ready, steady, go!
Humans!
She's got a kite.
He's got a Frisbee.

Wordlist

At the beach
a whistle
goggles
a towel
the sea
a flag
a lifeguard
There's a red flag.
I can't swim today.
I can swim.

Unit 7
a tracksuit
shorts
trainers
sandals
a skirt
a T-shirt
a dress
trousers
He's got a blue tracksuit.
She's got pink sandals.
Let's walk!
I'm hot.
My feet are hot.
Take off your boots.
Put on your sandals.
I'm wearing a blue and white T-shirt, purple shorts and green trainers.

Unit 8
play football
run
swim
play basketball
dance
ride a bike
do gymnastics
roller skate
I can swim.
I can't dance.
A river!
No problem!
Who's that?
He's got a message.
Follow Dickin!
At last!
Can you swim?
Yes, I can.
No, I can't.

CLIL Science: The water cycle
Ice is a solid.
Rain is a liquid.
Vapour is a gas.
sea
rain
vapour
cloud
snow
ice
evaporation
condensation
precipitation
collection

CLIL Science: Healthy eating
What's in the yellow group?
fruit and vegetables
meat and fish
sugary foods
bread and cereals
milk and dairy
Milk is good for you.
Cola isn't good for you.
Grapes are good for you.
Crisps aren't good for you.

CLIL Citizenship: Recycling
glass
paper
general waste
food
plastic
metals
Comics go in the paper bin.
Crisp packets go in the general waste bin.
Let's recycle!
A comic becomes a book.

CLIL Geography: Landscapes
Cliffs are on the coast.
Lakes are inland.
woods
a lake
a river
mountains
cliffs
a beach
inland
coast
Big Ben is man-made.
Cliffs are natural.

Culture: Food and me!
This is my favourite party food.
We eat sandwiches and crisps.
roast chicken
roast potatoes
a birthday cake
sweets
a restaurant
curry
chips

Culture: Sport and dance and me!
After school, I do karate.
I'm wearing white shorts.
I've got a bat and ball.
I can't do ballet, but I can jump.
play cricket
do karate
do street dance
do ballet
uniform
indoors
outdoors
performance

Festivals: It's Christmas Eve!
There are presents under the tree.
I hang my stocking.
Christmas Eve
a stocking
a fireplace
mince pies
a letter
a reindeer
baubles
Father Christmas

Festivals: It's Easter time!
There's yellow dye on this egg.
There are two purple flowers.
Easter eggs
decorate
paint
dye
pattern
a circle
a triangle

Song lyrics

Along the canal: The Road Safety Song
Look left, look right
Wait for the traffic lights
To change from red to green.
Be cool, be great
Stop. Look. Listen. Wait!
When you cross the road.

Walk on the pavement
When you're in the town.
Keep safe, be cool
Always look around.
Put on a seat belt
When you're in a car.
Keep safe, be cool
You're a superstar!

At the zebra crossing
Wait for cars to stop.
Keep safe, be cool
When you go to the shop.
Put on a helmet
When you're on a bike.
Oh! It's windy.
Hold on tight!

Unit 1: Let's go to Town Song
Hello, nice to meet you!
How are you today?
Welcome to my busy town.
Let me show you around.

Look, there's a post office
And a police station, too.
Look, there's a toy shop
Just for you.
Look, there's a school
And lots of cafes.
There are lots of playgrounds.
I play with my friends all day.

Look, there's a bookshop
And a clothes shop, too.
We can go shopping
And buy a gift for you.
Look, there's a school
And lots of cafes.
There are lots of playgrounds.
I play with my friends all day.

Unit 2: The Raft Race Song
There are ten people in the raft race today,
Ten people in the raft race today.
Let's count the people in the raft race today.
Are you ready? Hip, hip, hooray!

One, two, three,
Four, five, six,
Seven, eight, nine, ten people!
Hip, hip, hooray!
Let's find more people for the raft race today.

Eleven, twelve, thirteen,
Fourteen, fifteen, sixteen,
Seventeen, eighteen, nineteen, twenty people!
Hip, hip, hooray!
There are twenty people in the raft race today!

There are twenty people in the raft race today,
Twenty people in the raft race today.
Hip, hip, hooray! Hip, hip, hooray!
There are twenty people in the raft race today.

At the station: The Keep Safe! Song
Keep safe at the station everyone.
Hold hands with Dad and Mum.
Don't get lost. Don't run off.
Keep safe when the passengers come and go.

When you can't find Mum
And you can't find Dad.
Ask for help. It's OK.
Keep safe and enjoy your day!

Look! A police officer. Say hi.
Look! A train driver. Wave goodbye.
Look! Icicles and snow.
We're on the train. Off we go!

Off we go, off we go.
Chug, chug, chug, chugging in the snow. (x2)

Unit 3: The Food Song
My favourite food is spaghetti and grapes.
But I really love rice and cakes.
When the waiter comes,
I just can't wait
To eat my favourite food, spaghetti and grapes.

Waiter, waiter! Excuse me, please.
I don't like bread. I don't like cheese.
I like salad and lemonade, too.
But spaghetti and grapes are my favourite foods.
Yes, OK. I've got that for you.

Waiter, waiter! Excuse me, please.
I don't like soup. I don't like cheese.
I like sandwiches and fish, too.
But spaghetti and grapes are my favourite foods.
Yes, OK. I've got that for you.

Waiter, waiter! Excuse me, please.
I don't like chicken. I don't like cheese.
I like milk and strawberries, too.
But spaghetti and grapes are my favourite foods.
Yes, OK. I've got that for you!

Unit 4: The Shopping Song
We're at the market, at the market.
We love shopping at the market.
At the market, at the market.
What do you like at the market?

A key ring, please. A key ring, please.
Ten cents for a key ring, please.
An ice cream, please. An ice cream, please.
Twenty cents for an ice cream, please.
A postcard, please. A postcard, please.
Thirty cents for a postcard, please.

A doll, please. A doll, please.
Forty cents for a doll, please.
A comic, please. A comic, please.
Fifty cents for a comic, please.
A robot, please. A robot, please.
Sixty cents for a robot, please.

A car, please. A car, please.
Seventy cents for a car, please.
A puzzle, please. A puzzle, please.
Eighty cents for a puzzle, please.
And ninety cents for a very big ball,
One hundred cents, you can have them all!

Unit 5: I Love My Bedroom Song
I love my bedroom, it's so cool.
I can play with my toys after school.
I sleep in my bed and I sit on my chair.
I play my guitar and dance everywhere!

There's a desk in my room.
It's so cool there's a desk in my room.
I've got a lamp in my room.
It's so cool I've got a lamp in my room.
I've got a wardrobe in my room.
Oh yeah, oh yeah.

There are drawers in my room.
It's so cool there are drawers in my room.
I've got a rug in my room.
It's so cool I've got a rug in my room.
I've got a bookshelf in my room.
Oh yeah, oh yeah.

At the beach: Respect the Rules Song
Let's swim, let's run, let's have fun.
Respect the rules in the summer sun.
Come on, everyone, let's have fun.
Respect the rules in the summer sun.

Look, there's a lifeguard, can you see?
He's got a whistle ... 1, 2, 3.
Look, there's a red flag, can you see?
I can't swim today in the sea.

Look, there's a lifeguard, can you see?
He's got a whistle ... 1, 2, 3.
Look there's a green flag, can you see?
Come on, everyone, swim with me!

I've got goggles and a towel.
Come on, everyone, let's swim now!

Unit 7: The Fashion Song
There's a fashion show, a fashion show.
Let's all go to the fashion show.
What colour are your favourite clothes?
Let's find out at the fashion show!

He's got a blue tracksuit,
A blue, blue, blue tracksuit.
He's got red shorts,
Red, red, red shorts.
He's got white trainers
And black trousers, too.
They're my favourite clothes
And my favourite colours, too.

She's got a yellow dress,
A yellow, yellow, yellow dress.
She's got a purple skirt,
A purple, purple, purple skirt.
She's got pink sandals
And a green T-shirt, too.
They're my favourite clothes
And my favourite colours, too.

Unit 8: The Cool Sports Song
I love sports. I love sports.
I love to dance and run.
I play football at the beach.
It's great and really fun.
I love sports. I love sports.
I ride my bike all day.
I love sports at the beach.
Can you come and play? Hooray!

Let's dance at the beach.
Dance, dance, dance.
Let's play basketball.
Hip, hip, hooray! Let's roller skate.
It's so great. Oh yeah, oh yeah.
Let's swim in the sea.
Swim, swim, swim.
Let's do gymnastics.
Hip, hip, hooray! Let's play football.
It's so great. Oh yeah, oh yeah.

CLIL: The Good for You Song
It's the good for you song.
The good for you song.
Come on, sing along!
Let's find out what's good for you.
It's good for you, it's good for me, too!

Fruit and vegetables are good for you.
I like carrots and apples, too.
Salads and orange juice are so yummy.
Fruit and vegetables are good for your tummy.

Bread and cereals are good for you.
I like spaghetti and rice, too.
I like sandwiches, they're so yummy.
Bread and cereals are good for your tummy.

Milk and dairy are good for you.
I like yoghurt, do you like it, too?
I like cheese, it's so yummy.
Milk and dairy are good for your tummy.

Meat and fish are good for you.
I like chicken, do you like it, too?
I like fish, it's so yummy.
Meat and fish are good for your tummy.

But sugary foods aren't good for you;
Chocolate, sweets and cake, too.
Always listen to your mummy.
Too much sugar isn't good for your tummy!

CLIL: The Rubbish Truck Song
Here comes the rubbish truck.
Say hello to the driver, wave good luck!
Let's recycle our rubbish today.
Crash, bang, wallop. Hip, hip, hooray!

Comics go in the paper bin.
Cans go in the metals bin.
Glass bottles go in the glass bin.
Think before you throw it away,
So we can use it another day.

Plastic bags go in the plastic bin.
Vegetables go in the food bin.
Everything else is general waste.
Think before you throw it away,
So we can use it another day.